The Megalith Builders

Series edited by Paul Johnstone *and* Anna Ritchie

The Megalith Builders

Euan
MacKie

PHAIDON · OXFORD

For Professor G. E. Daniel

I am very grateful to Professor G. E. Daniel for reading over the first draft of this book and making numerous helpful comments and suggestions. I also thank Dr. R. J. Harrison and Dr. H. N. Savory for reading the chapter on Iberia and Professor C. D. Darlington for reading that on Interpretation. None of these people is of course responsible for the opinions expressed in this work.

Phaidon Press Limited, Littlegate House, St Ebbe's Street, Oxford
Published in the United States of America by E. P. Dutton, New York

First published 1977

©1977 Euan MacKie

ISBN: hardback 0 7148 1719 8
       paperback 0 7148 1728 7
Library of Congress Catalog Card Number: 77-75401

Printed and bound in Great Britain by
Morrison & Gibb Ltd, London and Edinburgh

Contents

Two that remain of some 150 massive standing stones put up at Avebury in the 3rd millennium BC.

Introduction

The feeling has always existed among archaeologists and prehistorians that the whole dramatic episode of the appearance, development and spread of the megalithic tombs of early Neolithic Europe is a phenomenon essential to the understanding of prehistoric Europe itself. These massive stone constructions—representing as they do great resources of manpower and of technical ingenuity and organization—appear at a surprisingly early stage in the establishment of settled life in Europe: in Britain, in particular, the first Neolithic farmers hardly seem to have established themselves in their new land before these ponderous funerary and religious structures were going up all over the Atlantic coastal areas.

How can they be explained? Were the megaliths the products of travelling bands of religious missionaries who fired the zeal of the peasant communities they converted and persuaded them to build special monuments? Professor V. G. Childe favoured this diffusionist view in *The Dawn of European Civilisation* and tended therefore to assume an outward spread of megalith builders from the more developed urban cultures of the eastern Mediterranean area. Or were the megaliths a form of natural development among recently settled farming societies—perhaps built to weld the pioneers together as a social unit—the independent invention of megalithic architecture being one stage in the evolution of each newly settled Neolithic community? Professor Colin Renfrew tends towards this view in the non-diffusionist interpretations which he sets out in *Before Civilisation*.

Is it right to think of the massive megalithic stones used in the cairns as their common factor, if there is one, or the peculiar rite of collective burial (use of the tombs as sepulchres over many generations) which is almost always practised in them? In that case, other types of collective graves and mausoleums—like rock-cut tombs and earthen long barrows—would also have to be brought into the discussion.

Questions like these, often debated in the past, inevitably raise the problem of how much can really be deduced from mute prehistoric structures, built by people who seem to have had no knowledge of writing. Regretfully, theories about the kind of societies which raised megaliths—and the social forces which produced their wide distribution in Europe at a specific point in Europe's prehistory—do not and cannot come from the archaeological evidence itself but only from historical records (non-existent in this case) or by drawing *analogies* with apparently similar modern peoples whom we can study directly. In other words, we have to understand how known societies evolve and change before we can hope to interpret what happened in prehistoric Europe from the scanty and partial fragments of evidence which have come down to us from those times.

One particularly new and quite different insight into man's past—based on the genetic effects of human habits of marriage and breeding—was given in 1968 by C. D. Darlington in *The Evolution of Man and Society*. This present book will for the first time weigh Darlington's conclusions against the archaeological evidence.

Understanding of the late stages of megalith building in Europe—the erection of the stone circles and standing stones—has been enormously increased in recent years by the work of Professor A. Thom on the astronomical and geometrical properties of these sites and by the excavations of G. J. Wainwright on the giant earthwork enclosures of southern England. The extraordinarily advanced things that now seem to have been going on in late Neolithic Britain and Brittany radically affect former interpretations of the earlier megaliths and will be considered here. At the same time, in the light of a survey of the whole megalithic province, some more ambitious explanations of these developments will be put forward.

But, just as any field of prehistoric archaeology must have social explanations fitted on to its data if its research is not to grow sterile, so should there occasionally be more than one such explanation for the really important archaeological material. Only if two or more rival theories exist can the ideal situation be approached where new evidence is being sought, old evidence re-assessed and all theories and hypotheses ruthlessly re-examined and tested against the facts with the object of deciding which of the two explanations is nearest the truth.

This book aims to assess two rival groups of explanations for the European megaliths—the non-diffusionists who invoke independent local invention and the diffusionists who suspect some kind of influence from the Mediterranean world and the Near East. It will concentrate on three features which either do or could provide direct links between north-western Europe and the Mediterranean in Neolithic times, and which therefore need to be explained whatever general theory one favours. They are the passage graves, the practice of collective burial and the development of relatively sophisticated practical astronomy and geometry. It will see whether a new general theory can be constructed to explain in human and social terms the appearance and evolution of the megalith-building cultures of the Mediterranean and of Atlantic Europe—one which will take into account as much as possible of the great variety of new evidence now available. The theory eventually put forward is based on the concept of a 'religious revolution' as a specific stage in the development of civilized societies and on the effects this could have had on prehistoric European society. The book is primarily intended as a sensible alternative to the non-diffusionist theories which are now becoming so popular. Part of the reason for their popularity is that there is no up-to-date opposition and this is an attempt to make good the lack.

Dating

Much of the argument about how prehistoric European cultures developed inevitably depends on which archaeological sites and finds are older or younger than others, and a clear understanding of the basis for constructing time scales for prehistoric peoples is essential. Twenty years ago the archaeologists of Europe had to work out their chronologies by finding links between the prehistoric, undated cultures north of the Mediterranean on the one hand and the historically dated urban civilizations of Egypt and, later, Greece and Rome on the other. The links with these civilized societies were often—except after the Roman conquest—extremely tenuous and ambiguous, yet in the absence of any other method they had to suffice.

But in 1949 Professor W. Libby of the University of Chicago worked out a new system of scientific dating which could be applied to archaeological material and which has revolutionized prehistoric studies. The method is based on the rate of radioactive decay of the unstable form of carbon (Carbon 14) and has at last given archaeologists a way of finding out how old things are which is quite independent of archaeological considerations. It is applicable to any site, no matter how remote from the ancient centres of civilization, and is limited only by the fact that after about 60,000 years the remaining traces of Carbon 14 are no longer detectable. The conflicts between the dates given by this new method and those worked out in the traditional manner have often been severe and have provided some of the more entertaining rows in the archaeological world in the 1950s, '60s and '70s.

The basis of the radiocarbon dating method is the biological fact that all living things absorb carbon from the atmosphere or the sea and convert this chemically to carbon dioxide, which is passed back again into the medium from which it came. Thus, during its lifetime, a plant or animal constantly exchanges carbon with the atmospheric or oceanic reservoir but after death this ceases. Thereafter the carbon in the dead tissue is isolated.

Most of the atmospheric carbon is the inert form Carbon 12 but a small proportion is the radioactive isotope Carbon 14, chemically indistinguishable from the first. Carbon 14 is constantly being manufactured in the upper atmosphere by the bombardment of cosmic rays so the proportion of the radioactive carbon in the air and in living things is maintained in spite of its instability. The Carbon 14 atoms are, however, constantly decaying to nitrogen at a fixed rate. The material has a half life of about 5,730 years which means that, of a given quantity of Carbon 14 which is not being replenished, half has decayed after about $5\frac{1}{2}$ thousand years, half *of the remainder* (a quarter of the original) after another $5\frac{1}{2}$ thousand and so on. After about 60,000 years the residue is too small to be measured properly.

Thus one can measure the radioactivity of a lump of dead organic material, compare it with that of modern organisms and by this means know approximately what time has elapsed since its death and since fresh Carbon 14 ceased to be absorbed by it. Fragments of dead organic material— charred or waterlogged wood, charred grain, pieces of human and animal bones, plant remains and so on—are frequently found on archaeological sites and the age of these, and of the site, can thus be accurately determined.

However, the age discovered is that of the *death* of the organism concerned and not necessarily of the deposit in which it was found: death may have occurred some time before the object reached its final resting place. For cxample, the date for a charred wooden beam from a burnt house or fort will refer to the cutting of the tree concerned when the fort was *built*, not to the fire that destroyed it. Indeed, if the wood is from the inner part of a large tree the age found may be many years before even the time of felling; only the outermost ring (bark) in a tree is alive and it lasts only one year. Short-lived samples like cultivated grain, small twigs or fresh bones are best for radiocarbon dating as they are not so likely to have been lying around for a long time before being buried beneath a subsequent archaeological layer.

Important too is the fact that the radiocarbon dates are not dates but *time spans*. For reasons which it is not necessary to go into in detail it is impossible to measure the quantity of Carbon 14 in a sample exactly. The final age arrived at is only a probability that the real age lies within a given span of time.

By the late 1960s hundreds of radiocarbon dates had been obtained for the prehistoric cultures of Europe and had caused some dramatic upsets in traditional ideas. For example, in 1954 the beginning of the Neolithic period, and therefore of megalith building, in Britain was confidently put at about 2000 BC but the Carbon 14 dates soon forced this back to well before 3000 BC. Just as the new framework was becoming established, however, signs of a further upset in the dating system were becoming apparent. It had long been realized that Libby's method depended on at least one fundamental assumption—that the amount of Carbon 14 being made in the upper atmosphere was about equal to the loss through radiocarbon breakdown and that this amount, and this constancy, had remained the same for the last 50,000 years at least. If the atmospheric reservoir of Carbon 14 had been substantially more or less in the past than it is now age calculations would obviously be thrown out: in the former case objects would appear younger than they should and, in the latter, older.

A test of these assumptions was devised in the late 1960s of such elegance and simplicity that it deserves a prominent place in the annals of the history of science. The use of tree-rings for archaeological dating purposes had been perfected some decades earlier in Arizona, using the principle that trees grow one new ring each year and that, according to the vagaries of the climate and the local environment, these rings vary considerably in thickness. A long sequence of rings will show a clear pattern reflecting good and bad growing years and this will be matched in other trees in the locality.

Collective burial, the use and re-use of a single tomb over several generations, was the megalith builders' practice in 3rd, 4th and 5th millennium Europe. At Bryn Celli Ddu (above) in Wales is one of the commonest kinds of collective tomb, a stone burial chamber entered by a passage through the mound that covers it.

By cutting a very old living tree a sequence of several hundred tree-rings, showing a distinctive pattern, will be linked to a known year, that when the tree was felled. If dead trunks are found showing the early part of the living tree's ring pattern in their outer rings the sequence can be extended backwards. Wooden beams in ancient buildings may eventually be attached to the tree-ring chronology and thus allow these buildings to be exactly dated. Ancient Indian adobe dwellings in Arizona more than a thousand years old were dated in this way.

To Professor Hans Suess and a few others it became clear that if one dated by radiocarbon a sample of wood whose exact age was known by a tree-ring chronology, then one would know exactly how accurate such a date was for that year. In effect one would be measuring the state of the atmospheric reservoir of Carbon 14 in the past. The long-lived, giant redwood tree—*Sequoia gigantea*—of California was used in the first experiments on these lines, giving sequences of more than 2,000 rings in some cases, and it quickly became clear that the radiocarbon dates did not always exactly match the real age of the wood: sometimes these were a little younger and sometimes a little older than they should have been, but usually by less than a century. However, the *sequoia* revealed nothing about the reliability of radiocarbon dating for prehistoric times, when no other equally comprehensive method of dating was available.

Fortunately a much longer-living tree was discovered—the Bristlecone Pine, or *Pinus aristata*, living high in the White Mountains of California—and this has provided the older, exactly dated wood which was required. The Bristlecone Pine tree-ring chronology has in fact been extended back more than seven thousand years into the past and there are living trees growing which are more than 4,000 years old. The wood is remarkably resistant to decay and there are dead trunks lying around which span several millennia before the oldest living tree. As a result of a long series of Carbon 14 measurements on this dated wood a comprehensive graph has been built up to show the equivalence between radiocarbon years and calendar years back to about 5000 BC and there are hopes of extending it back even further.

In this way, before about 700 BC, radiocarbon dates become progressively younger than they should be if they were an exact measure of solar years. The discrepancy is of the order of two centuries at 1000 BC and rises steadily until it is eight centuries in the fifth millennium BC. Thus to compare Carbon 14 dates with calendar dates it is necessary to convert the former approximately into the latter with the aid of the tree-ring graph, always remembering of course that the radiocarbon dates so converted remain as time spans and do not become dates in the historical sense of the word. Indeed there are several epochs in the past when, because of sharp fluctuations in the calibration curve—presumably due to relatively rapid changes in the level of the atmospheric reservoir of Carbon 14—a radiocarbon date can have more than one equivalent calendar date.

Another dating system has been devised, which can establish the age of a potsherd from the time of its firing. This is the thermoluminescence, or TL, method and, though slightly less accurate than radiocarbon dating, does give ages in calendar years.

Throughout this book the dating system used is that based on calendar years—revolutions of the Earth round the sun—and most of the radiocarbon dates mentioned have been converted to real years with the aid of the tree-ring graph. All such dates, as well as TL dates, are distinguished by having BC after them whereas uncorrected dates are written bc. The radiocarbon and TL dates for the sites and monuments in the book are crucial evidence for the theories propounded and as many as possible are quoted in detail in the text. For reasons of length, however, an appendix with a full list of them has had to be omitted.

Definitions

A *megalith* is a large stone used as part of, or as, a structure or monument. *Megalithic* describes a building made partly or entirely of such massive stones or boulders, without any cement or mortar. Strictly this term is a purely descriptive one and has no cultural meaning, since large stones were used for building at different times and in many parts of the world by people who had no links with one another. However, the title of this book does for convenience use 'megalith builders' in a restricted sense, confining it to those Neolithic and Chalcolithic (Copper Age) peoples of the western Mediterranean and Atlantic Europe who lived between about 4500 and 1500 BC and who used massive stones for funerary and ceremonial buildings and monuments.

Upright megalithic slabs forming part of a structure are known as *orthostats*. A *menhir* is a single standing stone while a *dolmen* is a free-standing megalithic chamber (which may once have been buried in a mound) with a roof formed of a massive capstone.

Collective or *communal burial* refers to the funerary rite which seems to be the thread linking the European megalith builders and some other contemporary groups. It describes a custom whereby burial chambers were used and re-used over many generations, the older bones often being stacked on one site to make way for fresh interments. Collective graves were cut into rock or constructed of wood as well as of megaliths and drystone walling.

A *chambered cairn* or *mound* is the commonest type of collective tomb in Atlantic Europe and can take many different forms. The two main kinds are the *passage graves* and the *gallery graves* (though the latter term is not so widely used as formerly). The passage graves can be built of drystone walling, or of megaliths or of a combination of the two and they consist basically of a round burial chamber in the middle of a round mound with a straight passage leading to the exterior. Some passage graves, particularly in Iberia, are made entirely of drystone masonry (except for the flat lintels roofing the passage), with a corbelled beehive dome over the chamber.

The gallery graves normally have a burial chamber consisting of a long, parallel-sided megalithic chamber, often inside a long mound, which usually opens on to one end of the mound.

13

Skara Brae, Orkney village of the 3rd and 4th millennia BC, was found buried in the sand that had engulfed it after its abandonment and in mounds of household rubbish that had been building up while it was still occupied. Its nine self-contained, one-room dwellings were stone-built and all except one, which might have had a stone roof, were probably thatched. Stone-walled passageways that connected them were once roofed with flat stone lintels. Whether the sea has always washed so close against the village is uncertain; trees found submerged in the Bay have not yet been dated.

Chapter I   **Skara Brae**

In the winter of 1850 a particularly severe storm battered the open coasts of the Orkney Isles, exposed as these are to the winds and currents sweeping round the northern tip of Britain in both directions. On the western coast of the largest island—known as Mainland—is the Bay of Skaill, a broad, shallow inlet fringed with dunes and defined at both its ends by rocky promontories. Over the years a mass of wind-blown sand had accumulated in the southern part of the bay and the violence of the storm, driving the waves in from the open Atlantic, undermined some of the dunes and washed away much of the sand. Thus was there suddenly exposed to view, at a place called Skara, a massive 'kitchen midden'—a thick layer of refuse up to 4·6 metres in height, composed chiefly of ashes but also full of shells and fragments of horn, bones and charred wood.

The first actual digging at Skara Brae, as it was later called, took place about ten years later in 1861 and was carried out by one William Farrer, then MP for Durham, who opened up some stone-built chambers and passages inside the great midden mound. These passages were all filled with sand and with stone slabs fallen from the walls: immense quantities of shells and bones were found and large amounts of ash interleaved with the sandy layers. Stone paving was found at the base of the walls. William Watt continued the exploration after Farrer ceased work and by 1867, when George Petrie published the first proper account of the work at Skara Brae, he had succeeded in clearing out a large part of the ruins and collecting a vast hoard of primitive implements. Petrie made plans of the ruins and was glad of this shortly afterwards when several parts of the exposed walls collapsed.

By 1868 four chambers or stone huts had been exposed and a fine haul of relics had been found and deposited at Skaill House. For many years thereafter the site lay undisturbed although in 1913 some further casual digging was done into a new hut by Mr. Balfour Stewart, a summer tenant of Skaill House, and one of his guests, Professor Boyd Dawkins.

Eventually, in 1924, the site was placed under the guardianship of His Majesty's Office of Works by the trustees of the estate of William Watt. Then, in December of 1925, another very violent storm struck the site, washing away part of the midden and damaging some of the stone structures. To prevent any more damage the present sea wall was constructed and the buildings further consolidated. This work was carried out from 1927 to 1930, and from 1928 involved the first proper archaeological excavations there, carried out by Professor V. Gordon Childe.

Childe uncovered two major new structures and investigated below the foundations of the known ones and most of the reliable evidence about Skara Brae is owed to him. Finally, in 1973, excavations were undertaken at the site by Drs. David Clarke and Anna Ritchie and two new trenches were dug through the surviving midden deposits. The new work produced the first radiocarbon dates for Skara Brae and preliminary accounts make it clear that much new information has been recovered, both about the material culture of the inhabitants of the village and about their diet and their natural environment. The suggestions made here about the kind of people who lived in the village, and about the way they obtained their food, will have to be judged against this much more detailed evidence when it is made available.

The site as it is now known consists of nine self-contained, squarish stone huts, the largest of which measures about 6·4 by 6·10 metres internally and all of which are connected by stone-walled passageways which were once roofed with flat stone lintels. The huts seem originally to have been constructed as separate, free-standing buildings. They were subsequently buried by the accumulation of the huge midden heap. This heap has the consistency of clay and contained the usual alternate layers of blown sand and midden of ash mixed with broken bones, shells and potsherds. It also covered the lintels of the passageways where these were preserved in position but did not overlap the walls of the huts themselves. The hut roofs, probably of thatch, must have projected above the general level of the mound.

The nine latest and most complete huts were not the first on the site. The foundations of at least four more were discovered partly hidden under their walls and these ruins lay on top of an even older accumulation of midden material. The only stone structure found with this earliest level was a hearth of exactly the same type as those found in the later houses and the finds too were of the same type in all the layers. There is little doubt therefore that Skara Brae was inhabited, from its earliest to its latest phases, by the same group of people, although several generations were no doubt represented.

The settlement

The general layout of the settlement so far revealed by all this work is fairly straightforward. Of the nine stone chambers in use in the village's final phase of existence, five lie to the south and four to the north of a main passageway running through the settlement from east to west. Five are substantial, squarish rooms while three are smaller: the size of the largely destroyed ninth room cannot now be determined. One room, Hut 7, set slightly apart from the rest, has a side passage leading south to it from the main alleyway, while another lies on its own at the west end of the village, beyond a small paved courtyard which was apparently open to the sky.

Among the megalith builders' ceremonial centres in southern▶
England, Stonehenge is architecturally supreme.

This isolated hut, known as Hut 8, had a stone hearth like all the other huts, but lacked the 'beds' and 'dresser' found in the others. In place of the 'beds' were two deep recesses in the side walls, of about the same size and perhaps serving the same purpose. The main door faced north, away from the main alleyway, and the hut stood quite free of the mounds of midden material which had buried the rest of the village. The excavation of its interior seemed to confirm that it was in a different category from the rest and did not serve a wholly domestic function. A small extra room, or annexe, was added at some stage to the south end of the hut and presumably a door was driven through the main wall to communicate with it. In this annexe were found huge quantities of heat-crackled stones, forming a solid layer on the floor, and many more were found heaped outside the hut. These stones were almost certainly pot boilers, heated in a fire until red-hot and then dropped into a pot containing a liquid soup or stew to heat it up: the sudden cooling of these stones in the liquid produces a characteristically crackled surface on them. A mass of ash was found on and around the hearth in the main chamber and contained quantities of charred whalebone, other animal bones and shells.

All over the floor were scattered small chert scrapers as well as cores and flakes of the same material. There were also some stone 'fabricators'—tools thought to have been used for striking flakes off cores in the process of manufacturing tools. The kind of domestic articles found in large numbers in the other huts were absent and an unusually large number of the stones of its walls and fittings were decorated with scratched and engraved designs in geometrical patterns. The roof may have been made partly of stone—as a corbelled dome—as many fragments of large slate flagstones were found lying on and embedded in the ash layer over the hearth. This more solid roof would be appropriate for a building in which large cooking fires were being constantly lit.

The singularity of Hut 8 is striking and the absence of evidence of flint- and chert-working and of cooking (as opposed to eating) in the other huts seems to suggest that this one served as kitchen and workshop for the whole community. Potting may also have been carried out there, judging from the heap of yellow clay found stacked behind some stone slabs. If this was so, Skara Brae may not have been a village composed of independent peasant families—each of which would probably have done its own cooking—but one which housed a single, closely organized community.

Hut 7 gave a clear idea of what happened at and after the abandonment of the village, an event which seems to have been abrupt and which sheds some light on the nature of the community itself. Childe found the walls well preserved, still standing up to a height of about 3·1 metres. Inside, just under the modern turf, a mass of stones was found that had fallen from the upper part of the walls and obviously represented the final dilapidation of the building, a long time after it was abandoned. This rubble rested on several feet of blown sand in which there was plenty of evidence of the last people to live there.

◀ *Five of the six bigger houses at Skara Brae were fitted with what look like stone beds and cupboards.*

On the hut floor itself was a layer 0·9 metres deep of clean, blown sand which must have effectively blocked up the doorway. Resting on this sand was a midden deposit of irregular thickness—it reached 10 to 15 centimetres in the northern corner—which contained ash, shells, and pieces of antler. Associated with this layer was a well-built stone hearth like all the others at Skara Brae. Childe concluded from this that some of the original inhabitants of the village returned, after the majority had abandoned the huts in a storm, to re-occupy the partly sand-filled house, presumably erecting a new light roof over the still-standing walls.

Since no layer of rubble from the walls was apparently lying on the floor under the sand—or anywhere in the fill except near the top   one wonders why these people did not dig out the sand and use the whole building again, incidentally recovering in the process many valuable objects on the floor. Yet they did not, and this first re-occupation layer was itself soon covered by more blown sand. A second, very thin midden layer then accumulated, which was covered in its turn by more blown sand. The third midden layer, 1·5 metres above the hut floor, then formed and in it were found shells and burnt bones. This was buried, a fourth layer of midden accumulated and then another layer of sand. At this point the tops of the walls began to collapse, depositing the layer of rubble already referred to. Childe noted that the meals eaten by this succession of squatters were mainly of game—deer and shellfish—in sharp contrast to the inhabitants' diet when the whole village was flourishing. In occupation layers of that period sheep and cattle bones were absolutely dominant and game bones extremely rare.

The square interior of Hut 7 measured about 5·2 by 4·9 metres across and was entered through a doorway equipped with a bar-hole and socket to secure the now-vanished door. The bar-hole led into a small adjacent cell which could be reached only from the passage outside, not—as with most of the other examples—from the interior of the hut itself. Thus the door, if secured, could only have been unbarred from outside the hut, as if it were a place of confinement. Another unique aspect of this hut was the raised gallery in the western half of its wall. This may have communicated with the upper level which is clearly visible in the main door—above the stone lintels—and perhaps with an upper level in the main passageway beyond: in this case any confined occupants could have been inspected and talked to from this upper level. None of the other huts had this arrangement, but there is no telling whether in fact it may have been connected with the later occupations of the room.

Inside the main room was a massive, rectangular, kerbed stone hearth with a stone block, presumably a seat, next to it. A long stone slab now lying on the floor seems to be a roof pillar fallen at the time disaster overtook the village; it had smashed a large pot as it came down. Against the right and left walls are two 'beds', long boxes made of stone slabs set on edge into the floor and about 1·5 metres long: each had an open 'cupboard' recessed into the wall above it. Other slots higher up in the wall near its top may have been for roof-supporting rafter beams. Next to the entrance, on the left as one goes in, is a solid block of masonry like a dais or table and opposite the door the 'dresser' with its two superimposed stone slab shelves supported by three monolithic pillars. A tank was set into the floor near the dresser, perhaps for water for keeping shellfish fresh and a cell inside the wall in the south-east corner may have been a privy, although no drain was found leading away from it. This contrasts with similar cells in Huts 4 and 5 away from which drains do run.

Projecting from under the wall behind the right bed was a large stone slab level with the floor underneath which was a grave containing the crouched skeletons of two old women. These may have been sacrificed to commemorate the building of the house or, perhaps more likely, they may have died normally and been placed there so that their spirits would protect the house and its occupants—a common practice among primitive peoples.

It was clear from the state of Hut 7 that it had been abandoned suddenly and Childe eventually concluded that a violent storm had torn the roofs off all the dwellings at once, driven away the inhabitants and half filled the roofless chambers with sand. The clearest sign of a sudden disaster was a cluster of bone beads found in the doorway with a few more scattered down the passageway outside. They had evidently come from a necklace which had broken as its owner squeezed hastily through the narrow door, the last few beads dropping off as she ran down the passage. Pots, implements and food refuse stood and lay on the floor and on the stone furniture just where they had been abandoned. Both beds contained pots and bone pins and ornaments and there was even the complete skull of a calf in the left hand one (this, the artefacts and the greenish filth found on its floor make one wonder whether these stone boxes were beds at all, at least in this hut). More pots and tools lay on the floor among food refuse and fragments of bones and shells. On the dais next to the door stood a whalebone basin, a stone mortar and two pots which had contained animal bones. A small whalebone basin holding a red pigment was embedded in the floor in the corner. A large pot stood under the dresser and another nearby while in the cell in the wall were found a pot and a hoard of beads and pendants.

That squatters returned to occupy Hut 7 at least, after the rest of the village had been abandoned, was plain from Childe's excavations of the midden layers. The excavations of the 1860s also seem to have revealed traces of activities later than the overwhelming of the village with sand. For example, in Hut 1 Watt found a contracted human skeleton in the sandy fill, about a metre above the central hearth, which could not have been interred until some time after the abandonment of this hut at least.

Links with the south

How was Skara Brae dated and why, despite its remoteness, is it more relevant to the story of the megalith builders of western Europe than might appear at first sight? When Professor Childe recorded his excavations in the early 1930s there seemed to be few reasons to suppose that the village was any more than a peculiarly Orcadian, prehistoric settlement of peasant herdsmen (no traces of agriculture having at that time been noted) bearing little or no relation to the outside world. The flat-based pottery found there, heavily ornamented with grooves and relief decoration, and some strangely shaped, stone 'cult objects' seemed unique, the products of a bizarre local development in northern isolation. The absence of clear dating evidence led Childe to deduce that the village belonged to the Late Bronze Age, which developed in about 500 BC in these remote islands.

But the story of subsequent revisions of the significance of Skara Brae is a remarkable one, though hardly clarified until now, and it may well be transforming our view of the settlement from one used by simple peasant families to one of far wider significance.

Some years after Childe's excavations, a very similar but much more ruined settlement was found at Rinyo on Rousay, another island in the Orkney group, by Walter G. Grant. This revealed both a very similar structural sequence to that found at Skara Brae and the same type of pottery and other finds. However, in a house belonging to the final phase of occupation at Rinyo was found a pot of the Beaker style of the Early Bronze Age. This immediately suggested that the pair of villages were much older than Childe had supposed and belonged in fact to the early part of the second millennium BC.

This was later confirmed by a series of radiocarbon dates for material recently excavated from the midden at Skara Brae. These ranged across about a century on either side of 2000 bc showing that the entire village, in its final phase of occupation, had indeed been used over a relatively short period of time.

Thus Skara Brae was shown to be a village built and lived in at the end of the great prehistoric age which produced the megalithic cairns and stone circles—the Neolithic.

In 1936 a new study by Stuart Piggott of some late Neolithic and Early Bronze Age pottery found on the submerged land surface at Clacton on the Essex coast demonstrated that the characteristic type of flat-based pottery found there—ornamented with geometric grooved patterns and a little relief ornament—was essentially the same pottery as that found at Woodhenge in Wiltshire and at Skara Brae in Orkney. A search through the sherds found on other archaeological sites of this period revealed that Grooved ware, as it was named, had been found quite widely but in two quite distinct geographical zones. These were southern and south-eastern England on the one hand and north Scotland and Orkney on the other, with very little in between. Since then many new Grooved ware sites have been located but the two-zoned distribution pattern of what was termed the Rinyo-Clacton culture (after the two type sites) has remained more or less intact.

In 1930 Professor Childe had suggested several analogies for the pottery he had found at Skara Brae with British prehistoric ceramics but the best match with other wares that he found was not from Britain but from Iberia. The late Chalcolithic (Copper Age) sherds from the cave of St. Joan d'Os in Cataluña were remarkably similar: not only could many of the

22

Flat-based, groove-decorated ware, peculiar to two distinct zones in late Neolithic Britain — north Scotland and Orkney, including Stenness (right), and southern England (above and below) — has now been found at Skara Brae and at the megalith builders' ceremonial centre at Durrington Walls. Radiocarbon dates for these two sites are the same and a chronological link between northern village and southern temple can be added to the ceramic one.

decorative patterns on the Skara Brae sherds be matched but also the techniques of making them were the same. However, a year or two later the discussion in his book *Skara Brae* ignored this analogy altogether, doubtless because Childe had by then concluded (wrongly as is now known) that a likely age for the village was much later at around 500 BC at the end of the Bronze Age.

Then the discovery of a Beaker at Rinyo in 1946 and the radiocarbon dates obtained from the excavations at Skara Brae in 1973 showed that the village was indeed a late Neolithic site. The Iberian links with its pottery could thus again be relevant. Links between the Grooved ware pottery of Orkney and southern England and the great megalithic tombs of the Boyne culture of eastern Ireland were obvious too, particularly in the remarkable 'spiral-and-lozenge' motif on a Skara Brae potsherd. This is repeated on stones of the New Grange passage grave in Ireland and on that at Barclodiad y Gawres in Anglesey. Similarities with French late Neolithic pottery were also noted as they were too with vessels found in the megalithic tombs of Spain and Portugal: the grooved ornament was especially close to the latter. The ornament on bone pins found at Skara Brae and Rinyo was also well matched in the Iberian megaliths.

Thus, hints that Skara Brae was something more than an isolated settlement have long been available. They have been reinforced in recent years by a series of remarkable excavations on large late Neolithic earthworks in southern England. Grooved ware had been found in quantity at Woodhenge—a ditched 'ritual' enclosure known as a henge and containing a complex circular timber structure—and when the very large henge earthwork at Durrington Walls—only a few yards from Woodhenge—was explored in the later 1960s great quantities of Grooved ware were found there.

Increasingly strong archaeological links with Ireland and Iberia as well as with the great ceremonial centres of the south of England, with which the village proves to have been exactly contemporary, make one suspect that Skara Brae had a distinct part to play in the story of the megalith builders.

Chapter II   Maltese Temples

The twin islands of Malta and Gozo possess between them an area of only about 308 square kilometres yet during their long history they have experienced three periods during which the island culture has flowered remarkably. At these times impressive monuments and constructions have been built there of a kind which, in the two most recent cases at least, were well beyond the resources of the native islanders themselves. The last two episodes were, first, from the sixteenth to the late eighteenth centuries when the islands were the headquarters of the Knights of St. John and, secondly, from 1783 onwards when they came under the protection of Britain and provided a base and dockyard for the British navy. During both these periods energetic foreigners came to Malta and built great military installations. But in the first great cultural flowering, far back in prehistoric times, the building had been apparently religious-based—a series of temples.

Although at first sight the prehistoric temples of Malta are not obviously connected with the contemporary megalithic tombs of Atlantic Europe (the primary objects of this study), either through their design or the objects found in them, there are at least four very good reasons for considering them here. The first is that the temple-builders of Malta must have developed or acquired very similar skills in moving and setting up enormous blocks of stone to those which were needed by the megalith builders of the European mainland. Secondly, a number of radiocarbon dates have become available for the Maltese archaeological sequence and have shown that the temples are far older than was at first thought. Thus the Maltese Neolithic temples, as Colin Renfrew was the first to point out, now take their place as the earliest known, free-standing roofed stone buildings anywhere in the world: the earliest of them moreover might be of the same age as some of the megalithic monuments further north and west in Europe. There is a possibility that the fore-runners of some mainland megalithic constructions were Maltese. Thirdly, Maltese and British archaeologists have between them built up a detailed and coherent picture of the development of the temple-building culture. Such a wealth of reliable evidence— based on modern techniques of stratigraphical excavation—is unfortunately not available for some of the other megalithic provinces.

The fourth reason for considering Malta here is a very important general one. Like the Iron Age brochs of Scotland and the great stone statues of Easter Island they provide a classic example of a remarkable cultural flowering in an apparently isolated and unpromising environment and they bring up fundamental questions about human society. Do these buildings represent the local evolution of an isolated Neolithic farming community up to an advanced level of proto-civilization—under its own steam as it were and without immigrants or influence from outside—or did the development of the temple-building culture follow the injection into the island of new talents and skills, perhaps of urban origin, by immigration and then hybridization?

The temple architecture

The megalithic buildings of Malta have excited wonder and curiosity for centuries but it is only during the present century—which also saw the discovery of the remarkable rock-cut hypogeum at Tarxien—that any sort of systematic study of these sites has taken place. About thirty temples are now known, mostly in ruins, varying in size from structures a few metres across to gigantic complexes such as that at Hal Tarxien which covers about 5,400 square metres. In general, the temples are stone buildings with rubble-cored walls faced inside and out with larger stones and constructed entirely without cement or mortar. The inner wall face in the better temples is often taken up higher, with cyclopean masonry of huge rectangular stones, and a variety of other megalithic furnishings can often be seen inside. The overall plan can be heel-shaped—or like a pentagon with three rounded corners—but the entrance is usually at the centre of the one concave side; this forms a facade backing a forecourt area in front of the building and the ends of the facade sometimes project like a pair of horns. The floors of the temple chambers and passages are usually made of massive stone slabs. Trilithon doorways—two monolithic uprights with a stone lintel—are often found leading to the inner chambers and sometimes a doorway has been cut through a single slab of stone. Inside the later buildings are ornately decorated slabs and blocks of stone, presumably serving as altars and screens of some kind, and the lower half of a massive stone statue was found in the Tarxien temple.

Evidence for the roofing of the temples is reasonably plain. Some of the rooms have preserved clear indications of inward corbelling in the massive blocks surmounting the upright slabs, as if a stone beehive dome had once covered them. At Tarxien the comparable corbelling can be seen to be semicircular with huge standing stones supporting the free ends; since these stones are only high enough to support the ends of four or five courses of corbelled blocks there would seem to have been a flat roof of wood and thatch on top of this stone foundation.

The decorated carved slabs found inside some of the temples confirm that roofs of some kind were employed. When these carvings were first excavated they were fresh and well preserved but erosion of the soft limestone slabs then quickly set in. For these carvings to have remained fresh and sharp while the temples were in use they would have to have been protected by a roof. Further evidence for roofing is seen inside the rock-cut chambers of the Tarxien hypogeum, some of which have been carved to imitate very strikingly the interior of a dome, made partly of megalithic blocks and covered with a flatter roof, presumably of wood.

This extraordinary megalithic architecture of Malta was, in part at least, the product of the type of building material available. Two kinds of rock suitable for building can be obtained on Malta—the Globigerina and the Coralline limestones; when freshly exposed the former can be easily cut but a hard patina soon forms on the cut surfaces which protects them unless further breaks occur. The Coralline limestone, on the other hand, is much harder, with a tendency to split into the flat slabs which are such a characteristic feature of the temples. The soft nature of some of the limestone beds also allowed the excavation in the solid rock of the numerous rock-cut tombs and of the unique hypogeum.

A convincing scheme of architectural development of the temples—from simple to complex—was worked out by Professor John Evans. The earliest temple is probably the smaller of the two at Mġarr. This is a roughly oval building measuring only about 10·7 by 7·6 metres overall with wall bases formed from relatively small stones. The design of the building is such that anything other than a wooden roof seems improbable. No horned facade is preserved in front of the entrance but it may have been destroyed by a later temple which was built up against it. The irregular shape of the first temple strongly resembles the local rock-cut tombs with their series of chambers hollowed out from a central area.

Once the idea of constructing a religious or funerary building had occurred, the development of temple architecture seems to have been rapid; the second one at Mġarr is larger and has already achieved a standardized trefoil shape with a pair of lateral chambers and one at the back, all of which open from a rectangular central court which is reached directly from the main entrance. The front of the building is a massive horned facade of huge megalithic slabs, one of which is nearly 3·6 metres high, and the outer wall face is also made of large stones though not of upright slabs. The chamber walls are of irregular stone blocks and squared megalithic slabs are used only for lining the passages and doorways. At Temple III at Kordin there are signs that the megalithic slabs were carefully dressed to shape.

From this stage onwards the aim seems to have been increasing size and elaboration and at the pair of adjacent temples known as the Ġgantija on Gozo the outer walls are built of enormous upright megalithic slabs and the larger building measures some 30 metres each way. The trefoil plan has been added to and in the smaller temple, probably built later, the front lateral chambers have become larger than the rear pair and the single central rear chamber has been reduced to a small recess. New features appear, such as large 'slab altars', one of which is carved with a spiral pattern. And fragments of a thick coat of clay still remained covering the inside of

27

the rough stone walls of the chambers; the clay itself had been covered with a thinner layer of limestone plaster and there were traces of bright red paint on that. The entire temple interior may once have been coloured red inside. The temple at Haġar Qim, although much added to in its later phases, shows how megalithic architecture was progressing, particularly in its enormous facade of upright slabs surmounted by huge, horizontal, dressed and fitted rectangular slabs. One can also see it in the use of regular corbelling or false vaulting in the chamber walls. Doubtless the Haġar Qim temple and most of the other advanced ones were roofed in this way. This building also shows that the temple plans were evolving in favour of increasing numbers of pairs of side chambers.

It is clear that by this time architects and engineers were thoroughly familiar with the potentialities of their limestone raw materials and also with the technical problems of moving, erecting and dressing huge blocks of stone.

Craftsmen skilled in carving and decorating stone must also have been making their appearance and their greatest achievements were certainly the temple complexes at Mnajdra and Hal Tarxien where the evolving megalithic architectural tradition reached its full and final flowering. Here decorated slabs, corbelled vaulting and trilithon and monolithic doorways are present in even greater sophistication. Stones covered with decorative pits are particularly common. The Tarxien temples consist in fact of three distinct though connected buildings which were presumably built in succession, one against the next. Not the least of the many interesting discoveries made there were the fragments of a limestone model of a temple facade from which a good idea could be obtained of just how imposing the great megalithic facade at Tarxien was when it was complete. The finest collection of carved stones in Malta, most of which are variations on the spiral theme, was found inside the first and smallest of the three Tarxien temples. The sacrifices of animals as part of the religious rituals performed there was deduced from the discovery of a mass of charred bones in the hollow interior of one of the altars and from a sharp flint flake —a sacrificial knife—still in its place in a plugged recess in the carved front of the altar. Also found in this building was the lower half of a huge stone statue of a female deity which has been interpreted as a fertility goddess.

The middle temple contained more finely ornamented megalithic slabs and, in one chamber, a slab carved with two bulls and a sow suckling thirteen piglets. Pieces of a huge stone bowl were also found here, and a striking pair of spiral carvings, like eyes, on the front of the high sill-stone in the passage leading to the second pair of side chambers, seemed to be guarding the doorway. Within these rear chambers were two exceptionally fine carved stone screens.

The Tarxien hypogeum

One of the greatest monuments of megalithic Malta is the extensive set of rock-cut chambers excavated out of the top of a hill of soft Globigerina limestone in the Tarxien suburb after which it is named. It seems that the

The second temple at Mġarr, one of Malta's earliest megalithic structures, is largely built of rough blocks of stone and has a small court (right) with three chambers off it resembling in plan the local rock-cut tombs where a series of chambers would be hollowed out from a central area. Haġar Qim (below) represents a later stage in the islands' megalithic temple architecture when huge slabs of stone were expertly dressed and the number of pairs of side-chambers was increasing.

original excavation of these chambers, which are on three distinct levels, was carried out over a considerable period of time and the rooms do in fact show different degrees of sophistication in their design. Of particular interest are the rooms on the second level which show, carved in rock, some of the remarkable architectural features of the later temples on the surface— trilithon doorways, upright slabs, megalithic facades and massive corbelled roofs with flat tops. Evidently the final great expansion of this so-called hypogeum took place late in the temple-building period when the most massive and elaborate megalithic constructions were being set up on the surface. The hypogeum was discovered in 1902 and parts of it were badly damaged—and more of it badly excavated—before Sir Themistocles Zammit took over the work in 1907. Most of it seems to have been used as a series of collective burial chambers, or ossuaries, and the remains of perhaps 7,000 disarticulated individuals were recovered during the excavations: the bones had been buried in earth which had been specially brought in and which filled some of the chambers and recesses.

The more elaborate rooms—particularly the 'holy of holies' on the third and deepest level—might also have had ceremonial functions. Traces of red paint and of spiral designs of the same colour on the walls recall the red paint of the Ggantija temples. The entire labyrinthine structure was dug out of the rock with antler picks and wedges and subsequently the surfaces of most of the chambers were smoothed with flint flakes.

Dr. David Trump, in his *Malta: an archaeological guide*, discusses the hypogeum and its social significance. He concludes that to find 7,000 burials inside the chambers was not surprising; if the estimate of about 10,000 for the Chalcolithic population of Malta is about right, then that number of burials could have taken place well within forty years. Yet the associated pottery suggests that the hypogeum was in use for six centuries 'so, tantalizing thought, there could be as many as fourteen other hypogea up and down the islands awaiting discovery.'

The assumption underlying this statement is that collective burial in impressive hypogea was the right of the whole population, from priest to peasant. Yet what if the assumption is wrong and only the priesthood, or some other ruling group, was entitled to such burial? In that case the 'fourteen other hypogea' probably never existed and an entirely different picture of the social context of the hypogeum would have to be built up.

An archaeological sequence

Thanks to careful archaeological work on Malta, it is now possible to fit the island's megalithic temples securely into a series of well defined and dated local archaeological periods.

At first the definition of the earlier of the Neolithic phases—before the temple-building phase—depended solely on the study of pottery typology and not at all on stratified deposits on ancient sites. However, Dr. David Trump's work at the small megalithic temple at Skorba between 1961 and 1963 revealed for the first time a sequence of early layers so that now all the

Megalithic architecture on Malta reached its peak in the 3rd millennium BC at the temple complexes of Tarxien (above, below left) and at Mnajdra (below right). Not only were massive slabs manoeuvred into precise positions but both interior and exterior walls were dressed and neatly jointed and many stones were decorated. Some were carved in relief (bottom left) and others were painstakingly pitted (bottom right).

phases of Malta's Neolithic and Copper Age periods are set in a reliable order and most are reasonably well dated by radiocarbon.

The whole of the Neolithic period (the Ghar Dalam and Grey and Red Skorba phases) and half of the Copper Age, or Chalcolithic period, (the Zebbug and Mġarr phases) apparently ran their course with no signs of any monumental buildings at all or of any of the rock-cut collective tombs that are supposed to have given rise to them. Only five of these tombs—those at Xemxija explored in 1954—seem to have been built in the Mġarr phase and even here most of the material found in them was of the following Ġgantija and Tarxien phases. More recently the dating of the early phases has been pushed back and the earliest settlement of Neolithic farmers on the island may have taken place before 5000 BC (there is no previous, Palaeolithic settlement). Judging from the tree-ring correction of the radiocarbon dates, the first Skorba phase had apparently begun by 4000 BC while the Zebbug phase—the first of the Chalcolithic period—is well dated by two consistent radiocarbon measurements that include the span 3800 to 3700 BC. The Mġarr phase must follow on at about 3500 BC.

It is in the following Ġgantija phase that the temples appear on the scene, many—like Skorba itself—having probably been planted on ground that had previously been cultivated or lived on. Nearly all the various kinds of megalithic constructions which were thought by Evans to illustrate a steady development—from simple trefoil temples he put in the Zebbug period through more complex temples with two and then three sets of chambers— are now seen to have appeared apparently together in the Ġgantija phase. This period has two radiocarbon dates, one of which may be a little too old, but it could well have started by 3500 BC and have lasted until 3000 or even till 2800 or 2700 BC. The lower limit of the temple-building culture was provided by a radiocarbon date obtained from charred grain found in the cremation cemetery at Hal Tarxien—the first phase of the Bronze Age— which was equivalent to about 2500–2400 BC. Thus the latest Chalcolithic temples of the Saflieni and the Tarxien periods (which include the only known six-apse building) had been built and used for some time, and all the temples on the island had apparently been abandoned and fallen into ruin, by just after the middle of the third millennium BC.

What is striking is that both the introduction of rock-cut collective tombs to the island, and the subsequent building of temples, appear relatively suddenly, and at a surprisingly early date in terms of calendar years, but on an island with a much older history of Neolithic settlement. Although the individual temples themselves need more exact dating by means of radiocarbon there is not much doubt that they began at least as early as 3500 BC and were thus being built and used both before and at the same time as the Old Kingdom period in Egypt (about 2800–2400 BC) and the contemporary Early Minoan period on Crete. They almost certainly originate before the unification of Egypt at about 3100 BC and are now of the right age to be considered as another aspect of the general phenomenon of megalith building in western Europe in the fifth, fourth and third millennia BC.

Chapter III   Iberian Tombs and Settlements

Neolithic and Copper Age sites in Spain and Portugal in the Iberian peninsula provide the clearest evidence for the origin and earliest development of the prehistoric people who practised collective burial and built megalithic sepulchres for their dead. They also represent far the richest culture of those created by the megalith builders of Atlantic Europe, while several of the sites reveal both cemeteries of collective tombs and, close by, fortified settlements. In other parts of the megalithic province there survive only the burial mounds, unless the Maltese temples are regarded as entirely non-sepulchral buildings.

Spanish archaeologists had long pondered the origin of the advanced, metal-using Chalcolithic cultures which were centred on such elaborately fortified sites as Los Millares and Almizaraque in Spain and Zambujal, Rotura and Vila Nova de Saõ Pedro, with several others, in central Portugal. Some of the fortified settlements in south-east Spain, notably Los Millares, are close to cemeteries of well-built passage graves of the same kind that form such an important feature of the megalith builders' culture throughout Atlantic Europe. And in many other aspects these Chalcolithic settlements show such a sharp break with the preceding Neolithic cultures that they were early identified as the small towns of actual colonists from the Aegean area or the east coast of the Mediterranean who had brought their urban skills with them. Their town defences consisted of layered stone walls with projecting bastions, a sophisticated feature which recalled Early Bronze Age settlements of the East. A motive for their arrival was found in the frequent nearness of the settlements to copper-ores; and abundant evidence of metal-working on the sites supported the idea that the colonists were prospectors.

Both V. Gordon Childe in the 1950s and Dr. Beatrice Blance, after a fresh survey of the evidence in 1961, agreed with a colonial explanation of the settlements. The metallurgical traditions, the town-like settlements with sophisticated fortifications and the new pottery—with Aegean parallels—all clearly showed that foreigners had created the culture. These views were challenged—along with almost all other explanations of prehistoric Europe which invoked some form of geographical movement of people and skills—

33

by Professor Colin Renfrew in the late 1960s. The archaeological details of the colonial hypothesis were questioned but a major argument against it was a chronological one. By that time the passage graves of Brittany were known to be extremely old; when corrected, several of their radiocarbon dates fell in the middle and latter part of the fifth millenium BC, far earlier than any dates available for Iberian passage graves. In the old scheme the origins of the tradition of collective burial in passage graves—so widely spread in Atlantic Europe—could be explained by the activities of the Iberian Chalcolithic colonists and by supposing that more barbarous and primitive versions of their traditions subsequently spread northwards, to France, Britain, northern Europe and Scandinavia. The fine, large corbel-vaulted tombs of Spain and Portugal could thus be thought of as ancestral to the Breton, Irish and Orkney tombs of the same type. However the new dates for the Breton tombs seemed to make this attractive scheme impossible and the chain of diffusionist links between the eastern Mediterranean and Atlantic Europe, by way of Iberia, was broken. An independent development of megalithic building in several different places was held to be much more likely.

Thus the Iberian evidence is crucial both to diffusionist and to non-diffusionist views of the origins of the European megalith builders. If a colonial explanation is favoured then the 'colonies' of Iberia, with their passage graves, have to be earlier than all the other collective tombs in order to be ancestral to them. If, on the other hand, the non-diffusionist view is correct, they should be later, or at least of a similar age. But *all* Iberian passage graves have to be relatively late if the latter view is accurate. If Los Millares and allied sites come at a relatively late stage in the evolution of cultures practising collective burial in Iberia then is it possible that the more northerly collective tombs could be derived from earlier Iberian forms? It is now clear from the archaeological evidence that the Chalcolithic settlements—however they are explained—are late in the Iberian sequence of megalithic tombs and that there are older Spanish and Portuguese sites which might be ancestral to the French and British monuments. Much therefore depends on the dating of the Iberian sites.

Before the megaliths

When it was that the Neolithic, farming way of life developed in Iberia can only be estimated because the radiocarbon dates concerned are beyond the present range of the tree-ring chronology. It is possible that it was in the sixth millenium BC. The change to the Neolithic way of life was a fundamentally important one and, as nearly everyone but the extreme anti-diffusionists agrees, involved the arrival of new kinds of men bringing with them the seeds of already domesticated crops and driving flocks of tame animals. Since the earliest farming sites so far known are in the Near East it is not surprising that the earliest Neolithic sites in Iberia and other places exhibit clear signs of an east Mediterranean origin. The oldest sites in eastern Spain are distinguished by the presence of Cardial (or impressed) pottery, characteristically decorated with the edge of the *Cardium* shell. This must

The temple facade at Ḥaġar Qim was probably once surmounted ▶
by stone slabs to three times its present height.

represent the westernmost limits of the steady spread of the earliest farmers along both shores of the Mediterranean, where the same impressed pottery is found as far east as the coast of Syria and the Balkans. This slow expansion doubtless involved hybridization at various points between the new farmers and the local hunting peoples, to create characteristic regional groups. On the whole, however, the Cardial cultures occupy a zone which environmentally was essentially an extension westwards of Near Eastern conditions which the early farmers could colonize without having drastically to modify their crops and animals, skills and equipment.

The Cardial culture sites in Iberia are concentrated on the east coast of Spain in the provinces of Valencia and Alicante with some further north in Cataluña. A few are also now known in Portugal. The Cueva de la Sarsa in Valencia seems to have had a stratum with nothing but Cardial pottery together with flint implements, which included serrated blades, ground and polished stone axes, saddle querns and charred grain. There were also some bone spatulate tools very similar to those found in the equivalent sites in the Balkans—those of the Starçevo culture—and assumed there to be spoons for collecting the ground flour from the querns. The serrated blades are of the type used elsewhere as sickle blades.

A similar site, also in Valencia, is the Coveta de l'Or where some charred grain gave two radiocarbon dates which are probably equivalent to a date at about 5500 BC in calendar years.

These early farmers in Spain are known mostly from cave sites in contrast to the open, sometimes fortified villages of the Cardial ware people of the central and eastern Mediterranean. The Spanish sites also contrast with those further east in having plenty of evidence of flintwork in the form of triangular- or trapeze-sectioned blades, scrapers, awls and trapezes of the local Mesolithic (Tardenoisian) form. This must surely mean that the immigrant farmers hybridized both culturally and probably genetically as well with the local hunting peoples.

The Almerian culture is the name given to the other group of early and middle Neolithic sites—open settlements on hilltops, in the province of Almeria (later to become the focus of one of the two technologically advanced Chalcolithic cultures of Iberia). At El Garcel were found a series of round or oval huts, partly sunk in the ground but apparently with wattle-and-daub superstructures. The material equipment of the villagers included a style of pottery apparently linked with North African wares, flint sickle blades, saddle querns, polished and ground stone axes with round or oval cross sections and stone adzes and gouges. The flintwork consisted of tiny arrowheads of local type, again suggesting that hybridization had occurred between immigrant farmers and aboriginal hunters and food gatherers. Material of this same early Neolithic character, represented by round-based pottery, round-sectioned stone axes and geometric microliths (miniature flint blades and points) appears in megalithic passage graves and dolmens on the western coast of Portugal some of which contained only single interments.

◀ *The superb finish of the interior of the rock-cut hypogeum at Tarxien.*

The burial practices of the early Neolithic people of the east and south-west of the peninsula show no evidence for collective burial at this stage, individual graves being the rule. Among the skeletons found in these early graves, and in the later communal tombs of Neolithic and Chalcolithic times, two kinds of skulls have been distinguished. The first is a 'robust' Mediterranean or 'Eurafrican' form which was doubtless descended from the local Mesolithic (pre-Neolithic) population, and the second is the skull of a shorter, slighter-built people probably derived from intrusive populations of east Mediterranean origin.

The earliest megalithic tombs

It is now almost certain that the rite of collective burial inside large megalithic chambers—usually hidden inside mounds or cairns—was established in Portugal before about 4500 BC. Two such tombs are the Anta 1 at Poço da Gateira and the Anta 2 at Gorginos, both near Reguengos de Monsaraz (*anta* is the Portuguese word for a megalithic dolmen or burial chamber). Although these sites were excavated in 1948 and 1949 respectively by Georg and Vera Leisner—before the era of radiocarbon dating—it proved possible recently to obtain absolute dates for potsherds found in them by the TL (thermoluminescence) technique. Both tombs gave simple grave goods of the kind found in early Neolithic sites like El Garcel and lacked the elaborate flintwork, schist plaques and complex stone 'cult objects' found in later collective tombs in central Portugal.

Anta 1 Poço da Gateira is a passage grave inside a round cairn about 12 metres in diameter. The central chamber is about 3 metres long and perhaps 2 metres wide and is built of massive megalithic slabs that stand up to 1·7 metres above the ground; they now project well above the cairn material which, one supposes, once covered the whole chamber. The Leisners' excavations revealed twelve plain, round-based Neolithic bowls and 23 ground and polished stone tools; half of the latter were thick axes with round or oval sections and the others were 'hoes' with rectangular cross-sections. There were also long, unworked flint blades and geometric microliths. Although the local soil had not favoured the preservation of the human remains the Leisners found that the pots and other finds could have been arranged in 12 separate groups as if 12 burials had been made inside the passage grave, presumably over a fairly long period of time. In this case each interment would have had deposited with it a pot, a stone axe and a 'hoe', an unworked flint blade and two geometric flint microliths. One of the potsherds gave a TL date of 4510 ± 360 BC.

Anta 2 Gorginos is another small megalithic passage grave. The 1949 excavations revealed two plain pots in the passage just outside the chamber and other sherds in the chamber, as well as an axe and a 'hoe' of ground stone, a geometric flint microlith, a flint point and fragments of two flint blades. In the passage was also found, at a higher level, a copper point. Only one burial appears to have been made in this tomb and that gave a TL date of 4440 ± 360 BC.

Pottery impressed with Cardium shells (above, below left) was characteristic of the people who brought farming to Iberia in the 6th millennium BC. Megalithic building, collective burial and plain pottery make their appearance in the peninsula in the mid-5th millennium among the descendants of the immigrant farmers and local hunters. Rock-cut collective tombs as at Alapraia (right) are an early 4th millennium development.

Since single burials were made in southern Portugal in megalithic cists—with the same simple early Neolithic grave goods (though sometimes without pottery)—it may be that the megalithic passage graves used by the practitioners of collective burial owe their architecture to an earlier, perhaps Mesolithic tradition. On the other hand, the fashion for megalithic burial chambers could have spread in the opposite direction—from the collective passage graves to practitioners of single burial. Only a series of absolute dates for the various forms of tomb will supply the answer. These early cists were apparently roofed with rough corbelling and buried inside a round mound and the objects deposited with the single burials include items like a stone axe and a stone 'hoe' with a few assymetrical, trapeze-shaped flint arrowheads. Among the passage graves of this region appear grave goods of a late Neolithic date including concave-based flint arrowheads and early forms of slate plaques with engraved geometrical decorations.

One of the larger and more elaborate megalithic passage graves in western Iberia having late Neolithic objects is the Anta 1 (grande) da Comenda da Igreja. It consists of a central chamber, formed of stone slabs standing up to 2·4 metres above the floor and roofed with massive capstones, and a passage 10·5 metres long. The whole was enclosed within a cairn.

Excavations of the monument in the 1930s produced a large quantity of varied grave goods, but again the human remains seem to have disintegrated. Middle Neolithic material included geometric flint microliths, ground stone axes with round cross-sections and plain bag-shaped pottery bowls. But there were signs that the tomb had remained in use for a long time: concave-based and other flint arrowheads were found as well as large flint 'halberds', more elaborate forms of pottery including a few decorated bowls (two with the 'eyes' motif) and many fine schist plaques with holes for suspension and fine geometrical incised decoration. There were also some schist 'croziers' and many beads of various forms and materials as well as a small copper rod. Sherds gave a TL date of 3235 ± 310 BC but, judging by the presence of early kinds of grave goods, this fine example of a megalithic passage grave could have been built much earlier, perhaps nearer to the fifth millennium and the time of the two simpler *antas*.

The way in which the Portuguese passage graves developed architecturally is shown by several sites in which a later form has been inserted into a mound next to a megalithic *anta* of early type. One of these is the Anta 2 da Comenda. Here the primary megalithic *anta* shows a typical early feature, not normally found north of Iberia, in which the tall chamber is closed at the front by a massive slab resting on the inner end of the passage sides. Next to it was built at some stage a more developed passage grave of the type that used to be called a *tholos*, under the mistaken impression that it was derived from the elaborate stone-walled and corbelled *tholos* tombs of Mycenaean Greece. The oval chamber has a wall made of many close-set, thin, upright stone slabs sunk into the ground. Traces of horizontal walling are visible above the slabs and seem to imply that a drystone wall once rose higher and that the chamber was once roofed with a corbelled 'beehive' dome instead of with a megalithic cover slab. The wall does not seem to be massive enough to support such a slab.

The Anta 1 da Farisoa, one of a group of seven, lies a few kilometres to the south-west and shows a similar pair of passage graves. Here the primary megalithic *anta* is in the middle of a round mound 20 metres in diameter while the later, slab-built and presumably corbel-roofed tomb was inserted into the mound next to its eastern side; the passages of both emerge from the mound together. The megalithic *anta* contained some middle Neolithic material—round-sectioned axes, plain pottery, schist beads and geometric microliths—but also some late Neolithic items like geometrically decorated schist plaques and some concave-based flint points. Sherds from the chamber gave a TL date of 2405 ± 260 BC. The corbelled passage grave apparently produced only late Neolithic material; it lacked geometric microliths and schist beads but did have one round-sectioned stone axe; it also produced a variety of pottery, long flint blades showing secondary working along the edges, several concave-based flint points and some decorated schist plaques. Sherds from the chamber gave a TL date of 2675 ± 270 BC.

In spite of the apparently slightly older date from the later passage grave at this site there is no doubt from the relative positions of the two tombs that it was put in after the *anta*. The long use of the megalithic structure, shown by the grave goods, presumably helps to explain its late TL date. In general several such dates ought to be obtained from collective tombs which have been used over many generations, in order to get some idea of the length of time that they were in use. One can only take the earliest date for each type as an indication of when the new form appeared.

In south-eastern Iberia, in the Spanish province of Almeria, collective burial inside simple passage graves also seems to have been practised at an early date. Unfortunately, however, there are no reliable radiocarbon or TL dates for the funerary monuments of this area so it is not yet clear whether collective burial in passage graves was established in the south-east as early as, or earlier than, in central Portugal.

It has been argued that here the appearance of collective burial coincides with that of many influences from the eastern Mediterranean and the suggestion is that the burial rite may have been introduced by new arrivals from Syria and Egypt. In Valencia and Murcia caves tentatively dated in the late 1960s to the fourth millennium BC—and perhaps now to the fifth—have given multiple burials accompanied by a variety of new and apparently exotic artefacts. Bone pins with segmented, cylindrical heads similar to Neolithic forms in Syria are frequent and are also found in southern France. They are also found in contemporary graves in south and central Portugal with late Neolithic schist plaques. The pottery consists of simple bag-shaped, shouldered and cylindrical vessels and from the Cueva de la Pastora has come a twin-lobed stone pendant which strongly resembles examples found in Predynastic Egypt (that is, the period before about 3100 BC). Plain, flat bone plaques have been found very like stone ones from

Neolithic Syria. Were the owners of these objects new settlers and introducing communal burial for the first time despite the fact that their tombs are in caves, rock-cut chambers and in open sites rather than in the megalithic structures later associated with the practice?

Further to the south-west in Almeria there are many tombs thought to be much earlier than the elaborate passage graves associated with the Los Millares settlement. These are usually small circular chambers of drystone walling from 2 to 3 metres in diameter and having no entrance. Upright stone slabs are occasionally used in their walls but they seem to have had light wooden roofs and not to have been megalithic in construction in any sense. These tombs consistently contain plaques which are evidently related to those of the earliest Neolithic culture of the eastern coast already described and they may represent a westward expansion of these people—or possibly one in the other direction. The plaques are plain and anthropoid or oblong and carved: the latter are similar to some in Anatolia and to the schist plaques from the late Neolithic tombs of Portugal. There are also flat slate plaques like those from Predynastic Egypt while the trapezoidal flint arrowheads and the rare flint halberds, it has been suggested, could derive from the same south-east Mediterranean source. Some of the tombs of this phase further inland in Almeria seem to be simple true passage graves and have short entrance passages leading to a round central chamber which was apparently corbelled over to form a stone dome.

The collective tombs

The walled settlement of Los Millares lies on a promontory formed by the river Andarax and a tributary, several miles from the sea and from the modern port of Almeria in south-east Spain. The settlement's extensive cemetery contains at least 65 passage graves and circular burial chambers, all built of drystone walling. There is no doubt that settlement and cemetery belong together and that they date from the Chalcolithic period of Iberian prehistory. There are a variety of tomb forms present of which the earliest are probably the small number of simple megalithic chambers with short passages. Most of the passage graves however have drystone-walled chambers—presumably once roofed over with a corbelled 'beehive' stone dome—with a passage built of megalithic slabs. When Louis Siret first opened some of these corbel-vaulted tombs in the late nineteenth century, he found traces of plaster bearing painted decoration. These may be related to similar painted decoration in some tombs in north-west Iberia and perhaps ultimately to the decorated stones of the Breton and Irish graves.

Many of the chambers show an architectural feature seen in the later Portuguese graves, in which the base of the chamber wall is formed of close-set, upright slabs. Sometimes the chamber is completely enclosed but more often a passage gives access to it; the later monuments tend to have the passage as well as the chamber built of drystone walling and to lack megalithic construction altogether. Many of the tombs have relatively long passages divided up into two or three sections by upright cross slabs ('septal'

The slab-lined and lintelled chamber of the Dolmen de Soto, a megalithic collective tomb in southern Spain.

slabs) in which is a large opening or port-hole through which access to the tomb could be gained. These and other features of the tombs are seen again in passage and gallery graves in various parts of Atlantic Europe. The covering mounds are always circular and sometimes have an outer revetment.

One of the Los Millares passage graves, no. 19, was recently re-excavated and yielded material for a radiocarbon date which turned out to be equivalent to about 3100 BC. This tomb had side niches in its main chamber like the larger side-chambers which are a feature of later passage graves in Ireland and Scotland as well as in Iberia. The remains of up to 100 individuals have been found in the tombs of this cemetery.

The finds made in the cemetery on the whole lack the earlier Neolithic material—except for those from the few megalithic chambers—and show that the nearby settlement flourished mainly in Chalcolithic times. Abundant evidence of copper metallurgy has been found in the nearby settlement, including flat axes, awls, chisels, saws and knife-daggers, and there cannot be much doubt that the copper ores in the mountains around were a major concern of the inhabitants of Los Millares. The military capabilities of these inhabitants are also well illustrated by the three or four outlying forts, evidently forward defences for the main settlement. From other evidence the Chalcolithic period in Iberia lasted between about 500 and 1000 years, ending at about 2500 BC.

In southern and western Iberia more developed forms of corbelled passage graves eventually replace the primitive megalithic *antas* and have produced a rich array of grave goods of late Neolithic and Chalcolithic types. Some of these tombs achieved great size. For example, the Cueva de Romeral at Antequera in Malaga province on the south coast is an extremely large passage grave under an enormous mound about 70 metres in diameter. The central chamber is built of corbelled drystone wallings and is 4·6 metres in diameter and 3·8 metres high from the floor to the underside of the massive stone slab which caps the vault. A doorway leads to an end chamber north-west of the main room which is also dry-walled. The long entrance passage, up to 1·8 metres wide and approaching the chamber from the south-east, has walls of drystone masonry and a flat roof of heavy lintels as well as signs of slab-built door-checks. In its great size, in the length of its entrance passage and in its side-chamber the Cueva de Romeral resembles some of the very large passage graves of Ireland and Orkney. The possible doorway in the tomb passage recalls that in Maes Howe in Orkney.

In central Portugal, around the estuary of the river Tagus at Lisbon, is a concentration of collective tombs of a different kind. These are chambers cut out of the soft limestone rock of the region which have yielded an exceptionally rich array of finds including many apparently exotic, imported objects not found elsewhere. Rock-cut tombs were used in several parts of the Mediterranean world in the fourth and third millennia BC—in Sicily, Sardinia and in the Aegean for example—and the appearance of collective graves in this form in Malta evidently inaugurated the development of the remarkable temple-building culture of that island. On the Tagus the tradition of collective burial inside rock-cut graves, as opposed to megalithic or drystone passage graves, was evidently strong and lasted at least until the end of the third millennium BC, into Beaker times. The influence of the passage grave design can be seen in some rock tombs, notably the Praia das Maças.

In the late 1960s it seemed that the earliest rock-cut tombs in Iberia might be in southern Spain and the Cerro del Greal in Granada province was cited as a candidate. This was a domed underground chamber 2·7 metres in diameter which was entered through a shaft from the top, which could be sealed with a stone slab. The numerous burials inside were accompanied by Neolithic objects of early type—including plain pottery and flat bone idols. Another such tomb, at Aljezur in southern Portugal, also had many skeletons with the plain, early Almerian pottery, stone axe-heads, bone pins (some with segmented heads), flint halberds and some slate plaques with the early geometrical engraved designs on them. This kind of assemblage is of the late Neolithic kind found in central Portugal, in the second phase of passage grave building there, and perhaps belongs to the fourth millennium BC.

However, one rock-cut tomb on the Tagus now has a TL date of 3930 ± 340 BC, which suggests that the earliest tombs in this group also go back to before late Neolithic times. This is no. 2 at Carenque, 10 kilometres north-west of Lisbon, where there is a group of three rock-cut tombs excavated in the local limestone and only a few metres apart. The Chalcolithic settlement, as opposed to the cemetery, at Carenque is not far away. Carenque no. 2 is a circular, domed chamber 4 metres in diameter. An entrance hole in the top of the chamber leads to a vestibule and so to the 5-metre long entrance passage. Grave goods from the three tombs included Neolithic flint arrowheads and blades as well as decorated schist plaques and hemispherical pottery bowls. There were also examples of the many apparently ritual and symbolic stone objects which were consistently deposited in the collective tombs around the Tagus estuary but hardly anywhere else. Examples of these at Carenque include a carved limestone object like a handled adze, a crescent-shaped decorated plaque, a curved, horn-shaped piece with blunt projections along the convex side, several decorated tapering cylinders and a strange, decorated oval knob (or 'pine cone') with a short handle projecting from one of the narrow ends. Some of these objects also appear in the local passage graves and one site far away in Orkney has produced similar things.

It is not possible to tell whether all the objects described are as old as the sherd dated to the early fourth millennium BC but it does seem clear that the Tagus rock-cut tombs began at least as early as those on Malta. It is also clear that, in this region, the appearance of practitioners of collective burial marks the appearance of other important new traditions—first the megalithic passage graves and, at almost as early a time as these, the rock-cut tombs with many unusual and possibly imported objects.

The pottery found in the Tagus tombs includes some novel styles which are not found elsewhere in the peninsula. These, it has been claimed, strongly resemble some Chalcolithic wares of the eastern Mediterranean, specifically those of Anatolia and the Aegean. Such vessels, known as *copos* to Portuguese archaeologists, have a dark brown surface wash on a light body and are often decorated with channelled or grooved lines. Both the colouring and the forms of the vessels are claimed to resemble closely the eastern wares. However the comparable Aegean Early Cycladic pots do not seem to appear in collective tombs but rather in cist graves with single burials so the significance of the resemblances with the Portuguese pottery is not altogether clear. But more information about the place of this grooved pottery—which may be relevant to the problem of the origins of some of the late Neolithic pottery of the British Isles—in the Iberian sequence is available from some of the Chalcolithic settlements.

The Chalcolithic settlements

The position of the supposedly imported *copos*—groove-decorated pottery—in the local Chalcolithic sequence was first clarified in 1959 at the bastioned settlement of Vila Nova de São Pedro in central Portugal. Having abundant evidence of copper metallurgical activities this site had in the past been claimed as one of the colonies of people of east Mediterranean origin. The relatively sophisticated architecture of the bastioned walls had also been held to support the idea that urban professionals were at work on the defences. It is therefore of particular interest that both at this site, and also now at the comparable site of Zambujal (also in central Portugal), there has been recovered evidence of clear sequences of occupation in which the building of the bastioned *castros* can be accurately placed.

The *castro* at Vila Nova de São Pedro consists of an irregular enclosure about 25 metres across surrounded by a stone-faced, rubble cored wall up to 6·5 metres thick; there is one narrow entrance in the south-west corner. The wall shows the foundations of 9 or 10 semicircular projecting towers or bastions and there is a strong suggestion of an outer wall, also with bastions, about 20 metres away on the north-west with yet another wall beyond that. This citadel seems much too small to be a walled town and must surely have been the castle or keep of a local ruler though no trace of a small defended settlement or town surrounding it has yet been found.

A single trench cut through the wall of the citadel on the south-west side in 1959 revealed a thick pavement of pounded limestone mortar on which the fortifications had been built; it looked like a suitably level and solid surface which had been deliberately prepared to take the weight of the walls. However the greatest discovery was made by cutting through this hard layer: for the first time it was realized that there had been an earlier occupation at Vila Nova de São Pedro, before the construction of the fortifications. In the same way the cutting confirmed what was already known—that the castro eventually fell into ruins and that a late occupation layer with Beaker period wares accumulated over the disused fortifications.

A series of walled settlements, some of them small citadels like Vila Nova de São Pedro
(above) and others much larger, proto-urban complexes like Los Millares, have been
dated to the later part of the period when collective tombs were being built in Iberia. Like
Los Millares, Almazaraque had its own cemetery of collective tombs nearby (below).

The material found in the various deposits and layers assigned to these three phases showed both that there was considerable continuity of tradition through each of the two main periods of the site's history and also that some quite sharp changes marked the transition from one phase to the next; (however these changes are not so marked at the comparable site of Zambujal, now under extensive and systematic excavation). For example, some pottery items—plain bowls, jars and platters—occurred throughout the first two levels as also did curious horned clay objects and clay plaques.

However the pre-castro deposits contained many objects which had vanished by the time the bastioned walls were built. Most notable of these items was the groove-decorated 'import ware' or *copos* which is such a prominent feature of the rock-cut tombs of the Tagus estuary and which plays such an important part in the colonial explanation of the Millaran culture. Sherds of this pottery were most numerous in the very bottom layer where there were also many charcoal fragments. Saddle querns were also present and the flint flakes were roughly made; any more sophisticated flint arrowheads were absent as were any signs of copper metallurgy. The plaques in these early levels were plain.

In the phase 2 levels—associated with the fortifications—the *copos* had disappeared and in their place were found decorated bowls of Los Millares type bearing motifs including the rayed circle. Also appearing for the first time were the finely worked, concave-based flint arrowheads familiar from the late Neolithic finds in the neighbouring passage graves and also large numbers of rectangular crucibles for melting copper. There were some small copper tools including awls but no Beaker period sherds were found. Beaker pottery only appeared, though in large quantities, in the phase 3 layer near the top—a deposit in which there were large limestone blocks fallen from the ruined rampart. Judging from the consistent set of radiocarbon dates from the site of Cerro de la Virgen, Granada, at which Beakers were present, the final phase at Vila Nova de São Pedro probably began at around 2500 BC.

Thus, at least as far as the innermost citadel is concerned, the period once known as Vila Nova 1—before the final destruction—is actually two quite separate phases each with a distinct set of artifacts which can be matched on other Portuguese sites. Phase 1 seems to belong to the latter part of the Neolithic period and phase 2 to the Chalcolithic. However, the impression gained at this site that the groove-decorated 'import ware' is earlier than the Chalcolithic castro is not to be taken as a general rule. The very similar bastioned castro of Zambujal, near Torres Vedras in central Portugal, is currently being excavated and there the 'import ware' is evidently associated with an early phase of the fortifications.

The appearance of many flint arrowheads at Vila Nova with the building of the castro is not likely to have been a coincidence; the walls were probably defended mainly by archers. At Zambujal—which is also a small citadel with outer walls—numerous embrasures were found in the innermost wall through which archers could have directed their shots at attackers in interlocking 'fields of fire'.

One impression which could be gained from the Portuguese castros, though not an incontrovertible one, that military professionals were at work designing and manning the defences, is reinforced by the situation at Los Millares in south-eastern Spain, the site which had its own cemetery of passage graves close by. The site occupies about 0·05 square kilometres on the end of a spur between two river valleys, the Andarax and a tributary. It was first explored at the end of the last century but since then the enclosed area has been severely mutilated in various ways. The most recent excavations could not—because of these disturbances—gain as much new information as had been hoped. What was plain, however, was that the line of defences, 275 metres long, which cut off the end of the triangular promontory, was composed of a stone wall about 2·4 metres thick equipped at intervals with semicircular bastions projecting outwards. There was also a gateway in it 4 metres wide.

Unfortunately no clear sequence of stratified deposits could be identified as at Vila Nova de São Pedro so it is not yet known whether the wall was added to a pre-existing settlement, as at the Portuguese site, or not. A fragment of charred wood was found at the base of the wall, close to its foot on the outer side and under debris which had evidently fallen from the fortifications when the site became ruined. It gave a radiocarbon date equivalent to about 2950 BC which might refer to this collapse, and to the end of the Millaren culture, or it might belong to an earlier period of the site's history. The latter conclusion might be suggested by a date of about 2200 BC for charcoal found in a comparable settlement of Almizaraque and attributed to the Millaran culture. The Millaran phase at Vila Nova de São Pedro might have gone on till about 2500 BC.

The list of finds from Los Millares is long and varied and shows well how trade flourished. From North Africa, or Egypt perhaps in some cases, came ostrich-egg shells and objects of elephant ivory such as combs. An ivory sandal was found, similar to a limestone pair from Alapraia in Portugal, and, as are some of the bone and ivory combs, like objects used in Predynastic Egypt. It has been suggested that the skill needed to produce the fine, pressure-flaked flint objects found here may well be derived from the Capsian Neolithic and from preceding cultures of North Africa which are noted for the high quality of their flint-knapping techniques. Plaster vases have shapes in imitation of ostrich-egg shells and the criss-cross decoration on a variety of objects recalls that on Capsian pottery.

Connections with the eastern Mediterranean may be seen in the curious horned objects of fired clay from Vila Nova de São Pedro which have parallels in Anatolia and perhaps also in the metallurgical traditions which, it has been suggested, could have come from the same area. However, a local evolution of copper-working in Iberia has also been suggested and Los Millares, situated among metalliferous mountains, would be a possible centre for this. Copper tools include daggers with a mid-rib on one face only—indicating that they had been cast in an open mould—or sometimes with two, indicating the use of the closed or two-piece mould. There were

49

also long, narrow flat axes or adzes, awls and even some saws of the same metal. The flat, tanged copper daggers presumably belong with the small amount of Beaker period pottery found at the site, which evidently appeared late in its long history, and some Early Bronze Age material also occurs. Trade is shown by the presence of objects of callais, amber, jet and turquoise and links with the Portuguese tombs and settlements are abundant and clear.

Most of the axes were of stone and the pottery also reflected the earlier Almerian Neolithic tradition. Many pots however were decorated, some with the 'oculi' motif of a pair of rayed circles. This motif also appears on 'idols' made from animal bones. Flint arrowheads were numerous, presumably again reflecting the defensive methods used by the inhabitants, as well as their practice of hunting. A peculiar local feature of the ritual surrounding funerals in the passage grave cemetery were the many *baetyls*, or small stone pillars, which stood in groups in the forecourts in front of the tomb entrances.

The belief that the Chalcolithic walled settlements belonged to a relatively late stage in the period spanned by the collective tombs in Iberia has been confirmed by a series of TL dates which have recently been obtained for three Portuguese sites. Serra das Baútas is close to the Carenque group of rock-cut tombs at least one of which was in existence by about 4000 BC. Two layers were distinguished in the settlement, the lower being of Neolithic age and the upper of Chalcolithic. The former, with some microliths, gave a TL date of 3100 ± 305 BC and the latter of 2650 ± 260 BC. Penedo de Lexim is another hilltop settlement in which excavations revealed two main layers of occupation debris. The earlier one was attributed to a late stage in the local megalith builders' culture while the later was thought to be Chalcolithic and contemporary with the building of castros like Vila Nova and Zambujal. The earlier layer gave a date of 3055 ± 290 BC and the later one of 2880 ± 280 BC. Radiocarbon dates, equivalent to ages early in the third millennium BC, exist for Los Millares and Almizaraque.

Chapter IV French Passage Graves

Before the megaliths

The makers of Cardial pottery were in southern France in the sixth millennium bc if one may judge from a radiocarbon date of 5570 ± 240 bc for the stratum containing these sherds at the cave of Châteauneuf les Martigues. But the Cardial cultures seem to have been limited to the Mediterranean coast itself. The first really successful Neolithic culture to be widespread in France is known as the Chasseyan whose sites are marked by abundant traces of agriculture in the forms of flint sickles and carbonized cereal grains. However, radiocarbon dates for the Chasseyan sites fall between about 3800 and 3000 bc, about the same as those for the Breton megaliths and similar to the earliest TL dates for the Iberian passage graves.

Neolithic farmers also spread into France from the east into the Paris basin and as far west as Normandy and Jersey. This was a westward extension of the great Danubian Neolithic province, the farmers of which occupied the light, loess soils of central Europe from the headwaters of the river Drave in what is now Hungary, northwards to Poland and north-westwards to the river Meuse and beyond. Danubian sites in Holland are as early as 5000 BC but the few available radiocarbon dates for late Danubian pottery in France and Jersey fall in the first half of the fourth millennium BC.

South-eastern France

The compact group of passage graves in south-eastern France lies mainly in the department of Hérault, west of Marseilles, and extends about 48 kilometres inland from the coast to the mountains. At the end of the nineteenth century the tomb at Collorgues apparently revealed a corbelled central chamber containing a number of skeletons arranged radially. More recently Dr Jean Arnal has shown that most of these tombs have dry-walled passages leading to rectangular chambers and that the material deposited in them includes leaf-shaped flint points or spearheads, together with arrow points: no metal has been found in them and no radiocarbon dates are yet available, but it is hard to believe that these passage graves were not built by people connected with the collective burial people of south-east Spain.

Lébous, also in Hérault, is a village fortified with a stone wall which is equipped with round projecting stone towers. The whole sub-rectangular enclosure must originally have been about 210 metres around the perimeter with perhaps 11 towers. This site, and a number of other unfortified settlements, is associated with the late Neolithic or Chalcolithic Fontbouisse culture, the beginnings of which are usually put at about the time of the first Beaker pottery, that is now at about 2500 BC. Lébous ought therefore to be somewhat later than the south and south-west Iberian fortified settlements, which are so similar in many ways, and it is tempting to see a connection between the two areas.

Brittany

Brittany has the greatest concentration of passage graves in France and, being about midway between the large number of these structures in western Iberia and a similar concentration on the east coast of Ireland, has long been thought to mark an important stage in the gradual spread of this particular kind of megalithic building. The fact that the Breton passages graves—in contrast to the other kinds of megalithic monuments there—are almost all on the coast is of course easily interpreted if we assume that their builders came by sea, or that they went from here by sea to other territories. The distribution of passage graves in eastern Ireland, and in the Western Isles of Scotland, must confirm the belief that their builders included a class of skilled navigators among their number.

However, the argument has been advanced that the Breton passage graves were an independent local development, appearing for local reasons and owing nothing to the Iberian monuments of similar type. Colin Renfrew has advocated this view, citing as powerful evidence the fact that the Breton passage graves have produced the earliest radiocarbon dates for such monuments anywhere.

Further arguments in favour of a local Breton development of collective burial, and hence of megaliths, have been adduced from earlier Mesolithic sites in Téviec and Hoëdic, both places in the Morbihan region of southern Brittany where megaliths of all kinds are densely concentrated. Téviec is a rocky islet west of the Quiberon peninsula where a midden deposit, up to a metre thick, was found containing black earth, large quantities of shells, many domestic hearths, several larger 'ritual' hearths and ten graves containing 23 skeletons. On Hoëdic, another rocky islet, there was a similar, thinner midden layer with hearths, with 9 graves containing 13 skeletons. The Téviec graves were partly sunk into the subsoil and were entirely covered by the midden layer. The material culture of both sites was poor and included Mesolithic (Tardenoisian) flints; the diet of the inhabitants seemed to have been almost exclusively shellfish with few traces of fish or game.

The graves at Téviec contained from one to six bodies and those at Hoëdic from one to three, and they have been interpreted as family vaults in which successive burials had been made. The larger 'ritual' hearths at Téviec

The practice of collective burial in Brittany is marked by two distinct forms of megalithic tomb – the passage grave (above) with its chamber set within a round mound and a passage giving access to it through the mound; and the gallery grave (below) whose rectangular chamber opens directly from one end of a long mound. In both cases the mounds have more often than not weathered away by now.

were usually on top of the graves and stone structures were erected over some of them. Parallels with the collective megalithic tombs are obvious, though it is not clear that the burials in one grave were successive, but, in the absence of radiocarbon dates, it certainly cannot be maintained that these poor hunters' sites by the sea, with their allegedly communal graves, represent the origin of the great Breton megaliths. From what evidence there is it is possible to deduce either that the Téviec type of burial was a local Mesolithic tradition in its own right or that it represents a copying of the new and impressive traditions of megalith builders who had established themselves nearby, apparently in large numbers. Proof of the survival into Neolithic times of parts of an ancient Mesolithic population—apparently still pursuing their hunting and food-gathering more or less undisturbed by the Neolithic farmers living not far away—has been found in the islands of Argyll and in the valley of the river Forth in central Scotland, and also probably among the Ertebølle people of Denmark.

The concept of an independent origin for the Breton megaliths is better supported by a remarkable series of fifth-millennium radiocarbon dates which have been obtained for several of them. These go back to about 4500 BC and are still the earliest such dates known for passage graves anywhere.

In Brittany there is a sharp contrast between, on the one hand, the high, round mounds containing central lintelled or corbelled chambers—*dolmens à couloir* very similar to the Iberian passage graves—and, on the other, long rectangular megalithic chambers set inside long mounds which may not necessarily cover them. This latter type, sometimes called gallery graves or *allées couvertes*, is much more widespread in France than the passage grave type and it may have its roots in the long Neolithic mounds of north Germany and Poland. The long mound tradition flourished in England and in the valley of the river Severn and in the adjacent Cotswold hills are many chambered 'gallery graves' very similar to the Breton ones.

Until recently it was not clear in what order the two distinctive megalithic traditions—passage graves and gallery graves—reached Brittany: both occur in their 'pure' form on the south coast but hybrid forms could show that the ideas of their builders were blended together at some stage. One of the largest and most impressive of these supposedly 'hybrid' megalithic structures is the great cairn of Barnenez in Finistère on the north coast of Brittany. This is a huge composite mound, slightly below the highest ground on a peninsula; the summit is occupied by the north cairn which is presumably older.

No less than 11 passage graves have been found in the long cairn, their passages approximately parallel and facing south-east. The cairn is in fact built in two approximately equal parts, the one forming the north-eastern half being the primary cairn and containing five passage graves. This part of the mound is on fairly level ground. The south-western half, added later with six more passage graves, is on rougher ground, which probably explains why there are several vertical revetments of laid stone within the cairn material, looking like buried wall faces. A variety of constructional techniques can be

The passage through the mound of the megalithic tomb known as the Table des Marchands in Brittany is exceptionally long. Its lintelled stone roof now only partly survives (right). Toppled over not far from its entrance (top) is the Grand Menhir Brisé, a huge stone which, like the many hundreds of others in Brittany, was probably first erected in the later part of the megalithic period and later than this tomb.

Many of the great stone slabs lining the passages and chambers of the Breton passage graves have designs pecked in them. Few have any meaning to modern eyes, if indeed they were anything more than abstract concepts in the first place. Rows of hooked lines looking like hockey sticks cover a stone in the chamber of the Table des Marchands (above).

seen in the chambers; some have corbelled 'beehive' roofs, others are roofed with a single stone slab. Since the passages all end inside the edge of the long cairn it may be assumed that a final enlargement of the mound was constructed to conceal the eleven entrances.

Finds were most numerous in the chambers of the secondary addition. They ranged from early Neolithic Breton pottery through to Beaker pottery of the Early Bronze Age. In the primary cairn, one chamber was completely sealed in ancient times by a filled-in passage. An irregular paving of drystone rubble was found inside on top of the primary earth floor and charcoal fragments from this surface gave a date of about 4600 BC, one of the earliest radiocarbon dates for a megalithic tomb in Europe.

In the secondary cairn at Barnenez material was found for three more radiocarbon dates. In one grave there were many fragments of charcoal among the finds which included early Neolithic pottery; the date of this is equivalent to about 4200 BC. In another grave the primary level in the chamber gave early Neolithic pottery but on this surface was a bed of stones which extended into the passage and which contained large pieces of coarse, late Neolithic 'flowerpot' vessels and Beaker pottery. Another grave produced a flat-tanged dagger of arsenical copper of Beaker type; the arsenical alloy recalls the Chalcolithic metallurgical traditions of Iberia from which, in one view, the first Beaker people may have come. A fourth grave produced charcoal but little pottery from its primary levels and the date of the former was about 4300 BC; the passage produced charcoal from a secondary level dated to about 3800 BC. It is not easy to cast doubt on the reliability of the contexts of the dated charcoal samples from Barnenez but it is true that the deviations of the radiocarbon measurements are quite large by modern standards and that the dates may be a century or two younger (or older!) than they appear. It is also possible that wood from older structures or deposits was imported into these collective tombs for some reason, thus making the charcoal against which the cairns have been dated older than the cairns themselves.

But it was, it seems, the excavation of the central chamber in the cairn at Île Carn—at Ploudalmezeau in Finistère—in the 1950s which gave the stratigraphical sequence and the radiocarbon dates which provided the vital clue for the construction of a Neolithic sequence in Brittany. The primary passage grave at this site—the passage of which meets the round, drystone chamber at the right instead of at the centre—contained four good quality, round-based middle Neolithic bowls (the earliest type of pottery found in the Breton megaliths) as well as six schist plaques, one flint blade and several struck flint flakes. The two radiocarbon dates for this assemblage—performed on charcoal found on and between the paving stones of the chamber—gave dates of around 4000 BC. A date of 4000 BC was also obtained from a primary passage grave—with short passage and circular chamber—at Île Bono in the Côtes du Nord.

Barnenez in Finistère, containing simple, 'classic' passage graves with round chambers and relatively short passages, represents the earliest form of collective tomb in Brittany and any explanation for the origin of the megaliths must account for this and also for the fact that later developments diverged from it.

Passage graves with quadrangular or square chambers seem to be one of the earliest local developments and Kercado, at Carnac in Morbihan on the south coast, is a good example. This tomb has a square megalithic chamber with a roof of flat slabs and the megalithic passage is also lintelled with slabs: the whole is set inside a round mound about 23 metres in diameter. Kercado had evidently been used over a long period since it too contained late material like Beaker pottery, gold plaques, callais beads and pieces of jadcitc as well as early Neolithic objects like round-based pots, barbed and tanged arrowheads, pendants and dolerite axes. There were also pieces of later Neolithic 'flowerpot' vessels. The radiocarbon date was obtained from charcoal and centred on an age equivalent to about 4680 BC although again the large margin of error—plus or minus 300 years—could mean that the real age was substantially younger or older than that. Île Gaignog in Finistère is a mound containing three passage graves, one of which has a circular chamber and the other two rectangular ones. The earliest Carbon 14 date from this site was about 4500 BC. Likewise the square-chambered passage grave at Mané-Carnaplaye gave two dates towards the end of the fourth millennium BC.

An interesting development is the passage grave with side-chambers—a form also seen in Iberia, Ireland and Scotland and in the possibly connected group of long cairns in the Severn–Cotswold region of England. Unfortunately the Breton examples have not so far yielded artefacts or carbon dates with which they can be precisely dated although the two examples on Jersey—La Hougue Bie and Monts Grantez—gave middle Neolithic Chasseyan material. Perhaps the well-dated Irish examples, falling in the late fourth and the third millennia BC give a clue to the chronology of these Breton tombs, which have a markedly coastal distribution.

Also belonging to this relatively early stage in the development of the Breton megaliths must be the occupation site at Curnic, Morbihan, which has since been partly submerged by the sea. The occupation layer included potsherds, flints, and polished stone axes of dolerite as well as many traces of hearths and burning; two radiocarbon dates from the layer were equivalent to about 4300 and 4000 BC.

Another group of tombs have exceptionally long passages and the best known of these is probably Gavr'innis on an island of that name in the Golfe du Morbihan; here the passage is 26 metres long and almost every stone upright is elaborately decorated with pecked carvings. The tomb at Mané Rumal at Locmariaquer, Morbihan, has a passage 9·8 metres long. Such elongated passages reflect similar developments elsewhere: in the later passage graves of south-west Iberia and in eastern Ireland, for example.

A different kind of development seems to have led to passage graves in which the chamber is scarcely differentiated from the passage, the whole

Abstract designs predominate in the Breton megalithic tombs (right). One of the few apparently representational designs is of a hafted axe. Most have a simple triangular blade which is probably stone (above). Others, although metal axes do not themselves make their first appearance in Brittany before the Bronze Age, have the splayed blade characteristic of the earliest flat axes of copper or bronze.

having a wedge-shaped plan as at Mané Kerioned at Carnac. The Roudossec barrow contains three parallel passage graves, the central one of which is wedge-shaped; one of the others has a side-chamber. The pottery obtained from this type of passage grave is not of the primary, bowl-shaped Chasseyan form but is a developed form of Neolithic ware known as the Kerugou style which, it is thought, arrived in southern Brittany towards the end of the fourth millennium BC. Wedge-shaped chambers are also found in Ireland and south-west Scotland.

Yet another form appear to be the *dolmens coudés*, or angled passage graves, in which the inner part of the wedge-shaped passage is turned through a right angle in the centre of the mound. As with the passage graves with side-chambers and other devolved forms their distribution is mainly on the south coast of Brittany, in the same general area as the primary forms, perhaps confirming their ancestry in the early, round-chambered type. The relatively late date of the angled passage graves is confirmed by the rarity of Chasseyan pottery in them and the abundance of the Kerugou vessels. The Goërem angled passage grave gave a Carbon 14 date late in the fourth millennium BC, confirming the relatively late date of the group. Another monument which contained late Neolithic material was that of Crec'h Quillé in the Côtes du Nord with a Carbon 14 date in the late third millennium BC.

The supposedly typical form of gallery grave has a long lintelled megalithic chamber the height and width of which should not vary throughout its length, in contrast to the passage graves. The enclosing cairn is normally a long one, either rectangular or trapeze-shaped; the latter shape is particularly common among the long cairns and barrows of the British Isles and northern Europe. The *allées couvertes* in fact vary somewhat from this basic design and are moreover found all over Brittany (though not much beyond it), thus contrasting again with the passage graves which are mostly on the coast. Some of the Breton gallery graves have a facade in front of the entrance, again like many British and Irish examples.

One view is that the Breton gallery graves are an alternative late Neolithic development of the same megalithic funerary tradition seen in the various forms of passage graves. The grave goods of the two groups are similar as is the carved ornament on their stones. Although no Carbon 14 dates are yet available for a true *allée couverte* the artefacts found in them are always of late Neolithic type, broadly dateable to the third millennium BC. However, it is possible that a separate tradition of long cairns with burial chambers is as old as the passage graves. The long cairn at Barnenez, built at about 4500 BC, might reflect this as also might the long mound of Mont St. Michel at Carnac in which were a number of megalithic cists: charcoal from one of these cists gave a similarly early date.

One notable aspect of the Breton passage graves is the frequent occurrence in them of designs pecked upon the megalithic slabs of passages and chambers. Most of the decorated sites are in the Morbihan, the region of southern Brittany which has the greatest concentration of passage graves. A hafted axe with a triangular blade is prominent among the motifs at

Gavr'innis; the blades of these axes are perceptibly splayed, a characteristic of the earliest flat axes of copper or bronze. Thus, although actual flat bronze axes do not appear in the Breton graves until much later—in the Bronze Age barrows—it remains possible that metal axes were known to the megalith builders of the fourth, or even the fifth millennium BC but were too precious to be interred. Flat metal axes were known to the Millaran culture of east and south-west Iberia at the same time.

However, most of the other axes shown have curved, unsplayed blades or are simply triangular in form and may be representations of the fine green jadeite axes often found in Breton tombs and themselves perhaps imitations of metal ones. Though copper awls, and even gold objects, have been found in the passage graves, particularly near the coast, most of such objects are as likely to belong to the Beaker period as to be earlier.

Some of the decorated passage graves of the Morbihan bear a symbol looking like a boat with a high prow and stern and vertical lines which could be masts. Here might be a hint of the skilled navigators and their ships which must have borne any migrating megalith builders through the Atlantic seas off western Europe. Other symbols have no obvious meaning, like the rows of 'hockey sticks' in the Table des Marchands at Locmariaquer and the various 'buckler' motifs—rectangular or ovoid shapes with lines like hair radiating from them. The pecking technique in decoration in megalithic graves is a characteristic which is rare in Iberia but found in profusion in the passage graves of eastern Ireland.

Chapter V   Irish Passage Graves

The relationship between the megalith builders of the British Isles and the original Neolithic colonists of these islands is less clear than that which we have seen in the western Mediterranean, Iberia and France and is potentially different. In each of the continental regions there is little doubt that the practice of collective burial appeared on the scene after an agricultural population had already been well established. There, the contrast between the new rite and that of the aborigines is quite clear from the archaeological evidence. In Britain and Ireland, however, there are almost no signs of Neolithic settlement before about 4200/4000 BC, that is the time when the first farmers seemed to have crossed the Channel and the Irish Sea. The only exception so far is the site at Ballynagilly in Ulster where three earlier Carbon 14 dates were obtained for charcoal from pits containing early Neolithic pottery and near the remains of a wooden rectangular house; the dates average at about 4500 BC.

By contrast, the earliest date for an Irish or British megalithic chambered tomb is that from the Monamore horned long cairn on the Isle of Arran, Buteshire, which was probably built shortly before about 3700 BC; another long cairn with a megalithic chamber at Lochhill in Kirkcudbright was built over a burnt wooden structure of about the same age. A good number of the collective graves which are found in the south-east and east of England have been dated and they also fall into the centuries following about 4000 BC. There is therefore a high probability that in the British Isles the practice of collective burial arose, or was introduced, at the same time as or very shortly after the primary colonization of these islands by Neolithic farmers. For this reason it has always been difficult, when considering the British and Irish evidence alone, to see really clear signs of any distinction between the two groups. The archaeology of the early Neolithic period does in fact consist mainly of the collective tombs, in both megalithic and unchambered cairns, and one needs to look at Iberia and the Mediterranean to see that there is a possibility that the barrows and cairns of the British Isles may be the resting places of a special group, quite distinct from the mass of the peasant population. Conversely, the British and Irish evidence is a crucial test for such an explanation.

Ireland has the greatest concentration of megalithic tombs in the whole of the British Isles, with an estimated total of well over 500: however more than half of these are peculiar Irish versions, not found elsewhere. In north-east Ireland there is a concentration of about 80 tombs, long cairns often with horned facades at the wider end and with long megalithic chambers opening on to this facade. These are very similar to a comparable group in south-west Scotland and to a few on the Isle of Man. The second group consists of more than 300 megalithic tombs which are probably peculiarly Irish derivatives from the horned long cairns. These 'court' cairns are scattered all over the country, the horned forecourt in them extended to form a completely enclosed oval space with an entrance in front, opposite the tomb entrance. The court cairn at Armaghmare, Co. Armagh, gave a radiocarbon date falling at the end of the fourth millennium BC for some period of its primary use while that at Ballymacdermot, also in Co. Armagh, gave one falling at the beginning of the second for a similar phase of primary use. There seems little doubt therefore that the court cairns are a classic example of local development and are on the whole later than the primary horned cairns, one of which, in Scotland, was dated somewhat earlier, early in the fourth millennium BC at the latest. Some Irish archaeologists nevertheless hold the view that the court cairns are the relics of a distinct Neolithic colonization of Ireland—one starting from the west coast rather than the east.

Finally, among the Irish megaliths there are something over 130 passage graves of the international type that is scattered along the coasts of Atlantic Europe. Most of these are grouped in four major cemeteries recalling that at Los Millares. They were first placed in a European context by T. G. E. Powell in 1938 and named by him the Boyne group of tombs after one of the best known cemeteries, set in a bend of the river Boyne in Co. Meath. In this group are to be found such internationally known, magnificent monuments as New Grange, Dowth and Knowth, huge passage graves, each having an abundance of splendidly decorated monoliths. Examples of the highest achievement of the megalithic architects and builders and of the stone-carvers, they pose in acute form the inevitable question—local development or foreign intrusion?

The passage graves
The central part of Ireland consists of a great plain which comes down to the sea on the east coast on a broad front between Dundalk in the north and Dublin in the south. Through the middle of the plain flows the winding river Boyne. Geographically the eastern part of the fertile central plain is a natural place for sea-borne migrants to settle, whether from Sandinavia in Viking times or, in much earlier times, perhaps from Brittany or Iberia.

The Irish passage graves show a phenomenon familiar from other megalithic sites in Europe. They have architectural similarities with those of Brittany and Iberia but the pottery and other objects found in them are of purely local Irish Neolithic type. In the few tombs which have been carefully excavated it can be seen that the burial rite itself is—in sharp contrast to that of most of the rest of the megalith builders' province—cremation and not inhumation. Presumably the tombs are still collective ones—having been used over many generations—but the rite of cremation must surely have been adopted from the local Neolithic population.

In the Carrowkeel and Loughcrew passage graves the cremated bones formed a layer 15 centimetres thick on the floors of the chambers and these were mixed with unburnt potsherds and bone pins. The remains of over 100 individuals were identified at Fourknocks I and there is no doubt that here again in Ireland are collective sepulchres which were used over a very long period.

The passage graves can be divided into four types on the basis of the design of their burial chambers. Type I includes the relatively small cairns with diameters of 15 metres or less and with correspondingly small central chambers only 3·1–3·7 metres in diameter; these are made either wholly of drystone walling with a 'beehive' corbelled roof or else with the corbelled roof resting on megalithic slabs. The second group includes the so-called cruciform passage graves with three side chambers as well as a few tombs with more than three. The cruciform tombs include the very large buildings at New Grange and Knowth and most of them are made of megalithic slabs with the chamber itself roofed with a corbelled dome. Most of the decorated passage graves are in this group. The third group includes smaller cairns which enclose what appear to be degenerate cruciform passage graves while the fourth includes the undifferentiated passage graves—small round mounds in which passage and chamber form a single gallery with parallel sides.

Knowth

Extensive excavations at the great mound of Knowth took place during the 1960s under the direction of Dr George Eogan and have shed a great deal of light on the Boyne cemetery and its development. The primary problem of the excavator was to continue to test the two alternative hypotheses then current about the Irish passage graves—that either the large, elaborate ones were the earliest and the smaller ones 'degenerate' and later or that the reverse was the case.

The great mound is an approximate oval in plan with overall diameters of 80 metres from east to west and 90 metres from north to south. Dr. Eogan's excavations soon revealed that it was surrounded by fifteen much smaller passage graves, nine of which were of the undifferentiated type (with passage and chamber having a wedge-shaped or rectangular plan). Of the rest of these smaller tombs three are certainly and one is probably cruciform and two are too dilapidated for their exact design to be recovered. One of these satellite tombs was partly overlaid by the cairn material of the large mound, suggesting that Knowth itself was the latest and most spectacular construction on the site. This seems to be confirmed by the three radiocarbon dates so far available.

The great mound at Knowth in Ireland covers two passage graves, their chambers lying back to back and separated by only three metres of rubble. Pecked designs on a number of the mound's kerbstones (top right, centre) as well as on many uprights and lintels in the chambers include spirals and lozenges, 'fans' and 'serpents'. Concentric rectangles on one kerbstone (below) are bisected by a line that is almost exactly on the median line of the passage at whose entrance it stands.

The first radiocarbon date for the main mound suggested that it had been built at about 3300 BC but this was for charcoal under the mound itself and might be too early. Another date fell in the mid-third millennium BC and is probably more reliable. Likewise charcoal from below one of the satellite passage graves gave a date in the middle of the fourth millennium BC but a later measurement on material from the mound above the grave suggested about 3100 BC. It seems fairly clear that the great double passage grave was one of the latest monuments to be built on the site.

Other large and elaborate passage graves have also been dated. That at New Grange was built around 3100 BC while that at Tara, ten miles to the south, at about 3000 BC or a little later. Therefore it seems clear that the really large and elaborate Boyne passage graves belong to the middle and late stages of the Neolithic period and are more or less contemporary with the Millaran culture of Iberia. They are obviously much later than some of the large Breton passage graves.

A ditch had been dug round the mound of Knowth in early Christian times and it ran inside the ring of elaborately decorated, megalithic kerbstones. The mound was apparently used as a princely stronghold at that time and it was honeycombed with the drystone, underground, lintelled passages known as souterrains. The ditch had destroyed the outer ends of the two passage graves which were not discovered again until 1967 and 1968. These graves were set back to back and opposite one another and their chambers proved to have only 3 metres of cairn material between them. The eastward facing passage was 35 metres long with a cruciform chamber at the end; the westward-facing tomb had a simple chamber and an angled passage 34 metres long. Both passages had megalithic slabs for their walls and roof and the lintelled roofs of both increase in height as the chamber is approached. The simple western chamber is entirely megalithic with a ponderous lintelled roof but the eastern one has a beehive-corbelled dome resting on orthostats, more of which form the three side-chambers. The height of the inner part of this passage was increased with drystone walling laid on top of the orthostats.

The right-hand side-chamber of the eastern tomb contained an exceptionally fine stone basin decorated with pecked lines. Another basin was found in the western passage grave, at the angle in the passage, but is not thought to be in its original position. Both temple-tombs must have been entered, and probably robbed, when the entrances were discovered in early Christian times.

At Knowth a large number of the massive kerbstones, many of the megalithic orthostats of both chambers and several lintels were decorated with pecked carvings. And the kerbstone which lay directly in front of the western tomb entrance had a motif on it of concentric rectangles which was repeated on the massive still-stone at the entrance to the chamber and again on a stone at the back of the chamber. This kerbstone also had a vertical line through the middle of the design which lay almost exactly on the median line of the outer, straight part of the passage. The motifs found included concentric circles, meanders, horse-shoe shapes and spirals as well as shapes and areas 'shaded' by pecking.

The great mound at Knowth was found to have been carefully and systematically built up with alternating layers of different materials and showed strikingly different colours. At the bottom was a turf layer, then in succession came layers of stones, shale, boulder clay, shale, stones, turf, shale, stone and finally shale with a capping of earth. The structure of the mound seems to be uniform throughout suggesting that the whole thing was built in a single operation and that the simple megalithic passage grave is contemporary with the drystone, cruciform one.

New Grange

New Grange is another very large passage grave mound, less than $1\frac{1}{2}$ kilometres south-east of Knowth while Dowth, the third of the really large tumuli in the group, stands about 1830 metres further north-east by east of New Grange. There are various other monuments and earthworks in the vicinity including two probable henge monuments and two standing stones—types of late Neolithic sites which play an important part in the second major phase of the megalith builders' history. It is also of great interest that New Grange itself is surrounded by an incomplete circle of standing stones, twelve of which only now remain, and is the only one of the three large passage graves in the Bend of the Boyne to have such a feature. The links, on the one hand, between the stone circles and standing stones— which form the bulk of the megalithic monuments of late Neolithic times in Britain, Ireland and Brittany —and, on the other, the megalithic chambered tombs of the earlier part of the Neolithic period have never been clear but here at least on the Boyne there is a direct connection between the two groups of sites. This link is evident again in the passage graves and ring cairns of the Inverness region of Scotland.

During recent work on New Grange by Professor Brian O'Kelly, aimed at restoring and consolidating the mound and the passage grave inside it, some fine charcoal samples were discovered above the lintels of the passage which have given three reliable dates for the construction of the mound and chamber. A fourth date was obtained for the turf layer buried by the mound itself. These dates all clustered closely in the late fourth millennium BC, just before, or at the beginning of, the most flourishing period of the Millaran culture in Spain and Portugal. Whether the stone circle was also built at that time is not so clear.

The great mound of New Grange is 12 metres high and about 85 metres in diameter and is defined at its edge by massive megalithic kerbstones, many of which are elaborately decorated. The long megalithic passage opens on the south-east side of the mound and runs in straight for 19 metres before opening into a cruciform, megalithic chamber with a corbelled, drystone dome rising 5·9 metres above the floor. The side chambers are lintelled at a lower level and the total distance between the back stones of the two opposed ones is 6·4 metres. Three stone basins were found in the chamber (which was first broken into by the Danes in the ninth century AD)—two in the northern side-chamber and one in the southern. No less than 19 of the orthostats forming the sides of the passage and chamber were decorated as were some of the kerbstones, including a fine one with spirals which lies immediately in front of the entrance.

When Professor O'Kelly was supervising the restoration of the entrance he exposed the lintels of the passage and, in doing so, revealed the nature of the curious decorated 'false lintel' which had long been partly exposed above, and slightly set back from, the main outermost lintel of the passage. It was found to cover a deliberately made opening or 'roof box' through which light could shine down the passage if the main doorway were blocked. The sides of the opening are of drystone masonry and about 0·8 metres high and support two lintels, the upper of which is the decorated one. A block of white quartz was in this letterbox-shaped opening which is directly in front of a gap in the massive lintels of the main passage. Careful measurements as well as direct observation on the 21st of December, revealed that a few minutes after dawn on midwinter's day the rays of the rising sun shine down through this letterbox opening, through the gap in the passage roof and right down the passage, across the main chamber and into the rear side chamber. Although the position of the solstitial sunrise has changed by more than a solar diameter over the past 5,300 years the box is wide enough for the phenomenon still to be seen today.

It is very difficult to believe that this phenomenon was not deliberately arranged in order to form a dramatic part of a ritual celebration of the winter solstice. Before the marks for the position and shape of the mound and the passage grave were set out on the ground, the line of the midwinter sunrise at the site must have been established by direct observation and marked, doubtless with a pair of poles. Probably a suitable line would be marked by a string or cord stretched tightly between these posts, to represent the beam of sunlight at dawn. The mound, chamber and passage would then have been built around this device. Only if the path of the sun's rays on midwinter's morning had been thus marked could the builders have ensured that none of the massive stones of the passage grave would block the narrow beam of light, only visible on the shortest day of the year. The arrangement at New Grange recalls the description in the Talmud of Solomon's Temple in Jerusalem more than 2,000 years later; there the equinoctial sunrises are reported to have shone through a metal disc on the eastern gate and right into the heart of the temple.

The mound at New Grange is slightly egg-shaped and it too may have been carefully designed and set out on the ground with the kind of measuring rods and surveying skills that were widespread among the circle-builders of a millennium later. The geometrically constructed egg shape fits the kerb of the mound very closely. The south-eastern part of the suggested geometrical figure is half an ellipse measuring 104 by 72 megalithic yards— the unit of length, equivalent to 0·829 metres, deduced by Professor A. Thom to have been used in Britain and Brittany to set out and design the

The corbelled stone dome of the eastern chamber at Knowth in ▶
Ireland.

stone circles. The opposite part of the figure is an egg shape formed of arcs of circles centred on the corners of two opposed, right-angled Pythagorean triangles measuring 10 by 24 by 26 megalithic yards: the radii of the arcs are shown. (The importance of the Pythagorean triangle is that the sides are whole numbers of whatever measuring unit is used and that the squares on the two shorter sides add up to the square on the hypotenuse, in this case $5^2 + 12^2 = 13^2$. Not many right-angled triangles fulfil these conditions.)

The passage and chamber run along a line very close to the axis of symmetry of this figure and indeed one would expect that the line of the solstitial sunrise would lie on this axis, if there were one. The finely decorated kerbstone in front of the entrance, like that at Knowth, has a vertical line running down its middle which was surely intended to mark the point where the axis of symmetry emerged from the mound.

Culture and chronology

In sharp contrast to the magnificence of the architecture and stone carving of the Irish passage graves—large and small—is the pottery and artefacts which have been found in them. The tombs at Loughcrew and Carrowkeel in Co. Sligo have yielded fragments of a peculiarly Irish decorated version of the general early Neolithic tradition of round-based bowls of the British Isles which has been named Loughcrew ware. This pottery is presumably that of the local Neolithic population, adopted by the tomb-builders if these were newcomers, and it doubtless goes back to the late fifth millennium BC. Some passage graves were still being used in the Early Bronze Age, judging by a Food Vessel of that period which was found standing intact in the cruciform chamber of one of the passage graves of the Carrowkeel cemetery. A settlement of the Beaker people was found next to the Knowth tomb but the passage grave seems to have been permanently closed before this was established. Several radiocarbon dates for Beaker period pottery in Ireland show that its makers arrived there, as elsewhere in Britain, in the mid-third millennium BC. Indeed radiocarbon dates for the Mound of the Hostages at Tara, Co. Meath, showed that this large passage grave was built in the first half of the third millennium BC, not long before the Beaker period.

Other objects found in the Boyne passage graves include long bone or antler pins, up to 41 centimetres in length and often with mushroom- or poppy-shaped heads. The latter are found also in the sites of the Tagus culture of Portugal, including the fortified site of Vila Nova de São Pedro. There are also stone pendants of various kinds and one peculiar cross-shaped stone object from Dowth, with pointed arms, recalls a similar implement found at Skara Brae in Orkney. Several plain stone balls also have analogies in the Skara Brae material.

The simplest type of Irish passage graves are those with relatively small, plain, round or polygonal orthostatic chambers which are roofed with corbelled, drystone domes. At present none of these have been dated by radiocarbon so it is not known for certain that they are much older than the

◀ *A single massive capstone, once covered in a mound, roofs the chamber of a small megalith tomb in Wales.*

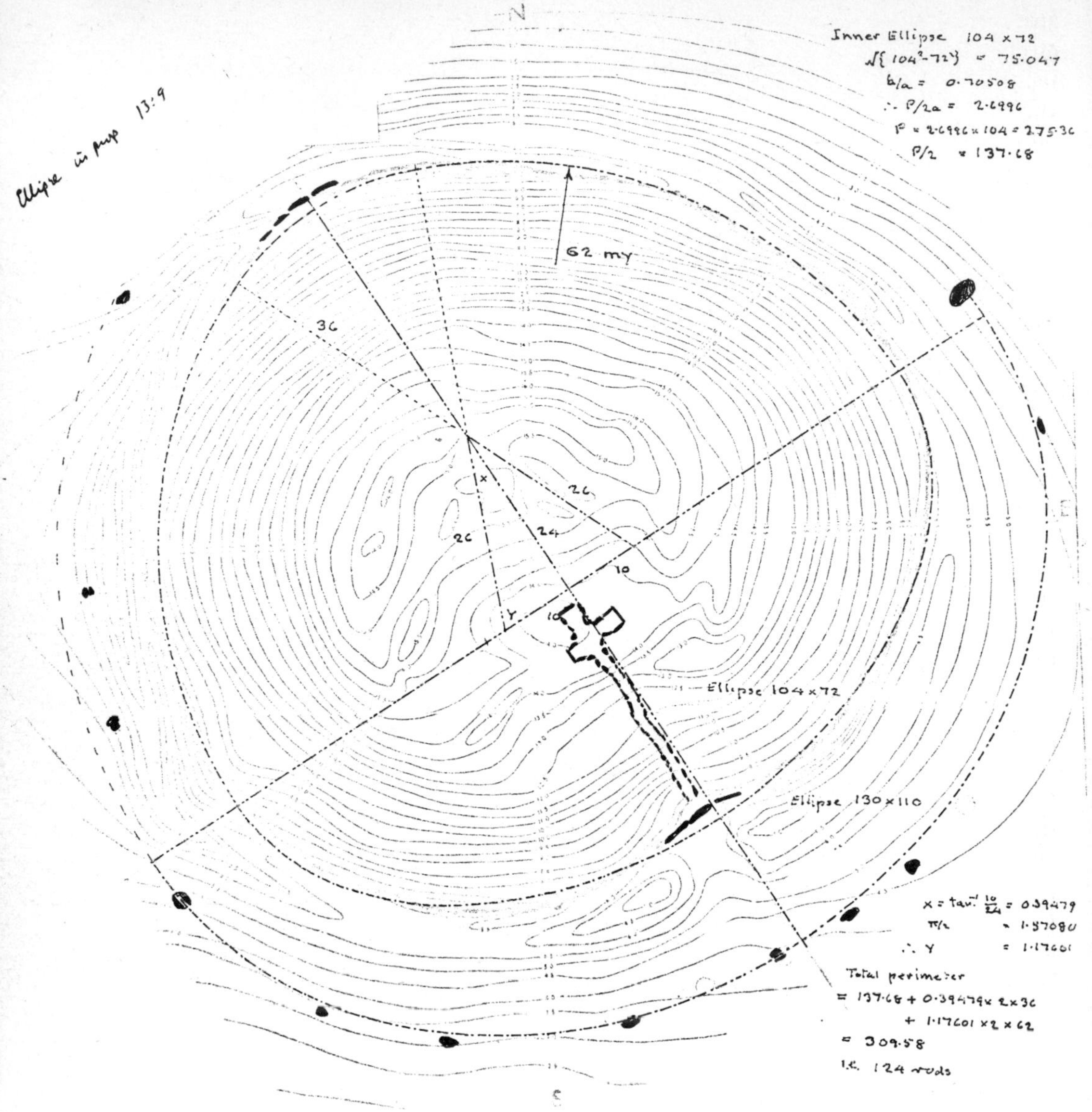
N
Inner Ellipse 104 x 72
√{104²-72²} = 75.047
b/a = 0.70508
∴ P/2a = 2.6996
P = 2.6996 x 104 = 275.36
P/2 = 137.68
Ellipse in prop 13:9
62 mY
36
X
26
26
24
10
Y
10
Ellipse 104 x 72
Ellipse 130 x 110
E
x = tan⁻¹ 10/24 = 0.39479
π/2 = 1.57080
∴ Y = 1.17601
Total perimeter
= 137.68 + 0.39479 x 2 x 36
+ 1.17601 x 2 x 62
= 309.58
i.e. 124 rods
S

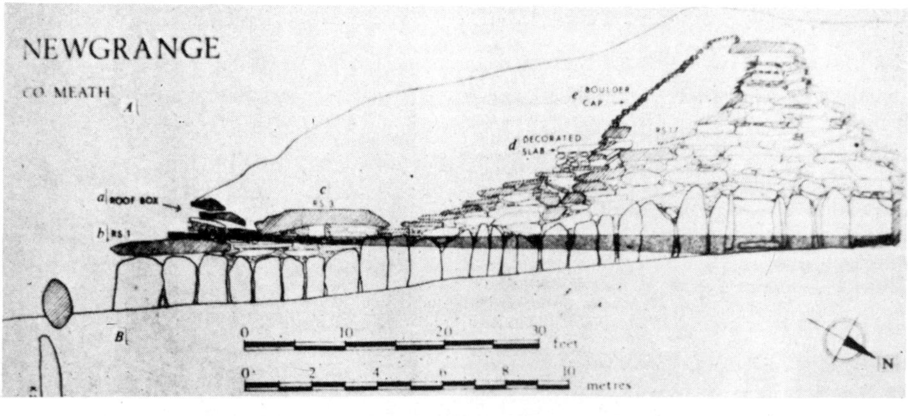
NEWGRANGE
CO. MEATH
A
a ROOF BOX
b RS 1
c RS 3
d DECORATED SLAB
e BOULDER CAP
B
0 10 20 30 feet
0 2 4 6 8 10 metres
N

Ireland has well over 500 megalithic tombs ranging from relatively small cairns (right) to elaborately planned and decorated structures like Knowth or New Grange (above). The plan of New Grange (top left) appears to be as carefully calculated on certain geometrical principles as the stone circles of the later half of the 3rd millennium BC. The south-eastern part of the egg-shaped figure formed by its mound is half an ellipse; the arcs of circles centred on the corners of two opposed right-angled Pythagorean triangles bound the other side. Passage and chamber lie along the axis of symmetry of the site and are illuminated by the midwinter solstitial sunrise shining through a purpose-built gap in the roof ('roof box' on the section, bottom left).

giant monuments like New Grange and the rest though it seems probable. The earlier date of the small satellite passage grave at Knowth seems to confirm that the large cruciform structures with very long passages are a relatively late development. New Grange should be contemporary with, or not much older than, the Chalcolithic Millaran culture of Iberia, another place where tombs with very long passages seem to be a late development.

Chapter VI British Collective Tombs

Few passage graves in England, Wales or Scotland have yet been dated by the radiocarbon method so it is not clear when the first was built. However, the pottery and artefacts found in them often include forms which are classified as early Neolithic so it may reasonably be assumed that the cairns were beginning to be built not long after the first Neolithic settlement of Britain. A whole range of radiocarbon dates for other kinds of early Neolithic sites allows a fairly exact estimate that this first colonization took place towards the end of the fifth millennium BC. All the long barrows, chambered cairns and other relevant sites of this early period which have been radiocarbon-dated fall into a period starting soon after about 4200 BC—and the dates are scattered fairly evenly over the millennium following. Only at Ballynagilly in Ireland is there a suggestion of an earlier Neolithic occupation. The oldest date so far obtained for a megalithic cairn in Britain comes from Monamore in the Isle of Arran, Buteshire, a horned 'gallery grave' which was built early in the fourth millennium BC and continued in use at least till the beginning of the third millennium. Another long cairn at Glenvoidean in Bute gave a slightly later date in the mid-fourth millennium BC for a deposit of charcoal in the megalithic burial chamber.

The passage graves themselves probably went through several stages of local development and, judging from the sequences established in Iberia, Ireland and Brittany, the earliest would have been small, simple structures and the later ones—built when the skills and confidence of the builders had increased as the result of many generations of experience–more ambitious and elaborate. There is sufficient evidence of the steady improvement in the building skills of the collective burial people elsewhere for there to be little doubt that magnificent structures like the Maes Howe passage grave or the Blackhammer stalled cairn—both in Orkney—come in the middle or near the end of a long tradition of drystone and megalithic architecture. In this at least there is no need to disagree with the anti-diffusionist interpretations.

The distribution of all the collective graves in Britain is striking. The passage graves are heavily concentrated in the far north—in the Hebrides, the northern tip of mainland Scotland and in the northern Islands; those in other coastal regions of the Atlantic or the Irish Sea—such as south-west Scotland, Wales, the Isle of Man or the Scilly Isles—are few and scattered. By contrast the other major forms of megalithic tombs—the long, sometimes horned, cairns—are heavily concentrated in the two other western regions of megalith-building, around the estuary of the river Severn in south-west England and in Buteshire and Argyllshire in south-west Scotland. They also occur in Caithness, mixed with the passage graves and forming some curious hybrids. Linked with these long cairns are the very similar unchambered long barrows, found mainly in southern and eastern England and south-eastern Scotland—regions where massive blocks of stone suitable for megalithic burial chambers are usually hard to obtain. Finally, there are widely scattered, simple megalithic chambers called portal dolmens which have been shown to be potentially very important in the context of the origin of the more complex structures.

It is important to remember that, where the evidence has been unravelled by careful excavation, the vast majority of these various kinds of early Neolithic graves—earthen long barrows, portal dolmens, long chambered cairns and passage graves—were used for collective burial in the sense that people were interred on the same sites over a long period. Time and again the bones of the latest burials appear articulated, fresh-looking and undisturbed (and occasionally accompanied by late Neolithic or Early Bronze Age grave goods) and the earlier bones disturbed, worn and disarticulated. Most of the grave goods consist of early and middle Neolithic pottery and stone and flint tools. A few examples have been found of Neolithic graves which are obvious single interments.

One of the clearest examples of long use was seen in the Monamore chambered cairn in the Isle of Arran, a small wedge-shaped cairn with a shallow, curved facade and a megalithic gallery with three compartments. Excavations in 1961 in the forecourt area revealed that dust seems to have blown into the forecourt area during the time the cairn was used as a tomb, gradually filling up the area in front of the entrance to a maximum depth of 1·2 metres. Funeral fires were lit in the forecourt at different times and the remains of these were thus buried under distinct levels of dust, one beneath the other. The oldest and youngest of these fires were dated by radiocarbon and the former proved to date to about 4000 BC and the latter to about 2900 BC. Shortly after the latest fire was lit the tomb was finally blocked up. Other tombs, some of which are described later in this chapter, show clear archaeological evidence for a similar long period of use.

Long barrows
On the chalklands of southern, south-eastern and eastern England are found scores of Neolithic long barrows—huge mounds of chalk and earth, flanked by parallel quarry ditches and covering a cluster of bodies that had clearly been dead for varying lengths of time and left lying exposed to the air before being finally buried.The barrows are not horned but wedge-shaped, with squared ends. The burials are usually under the wider and higher end.

West Kennett (above) is one of about 170 collective burial places grouped in the vicinity of the Severn estuary in southern England. Like most of its neighbours, West Kennett is trapeze-shaped, with one wide end (below) where entrance is made directly into a straight megalithic gallery with side-chambers (right). The bodies in the tomb had been left to decay completely then their bones had been stacked up in rows.

At Wayland's Smithy in southern England (above), a mid-4th millennium, trapeze-shaped mound with megalithic gallery and side-chambers was built on the site of an earlier, wooden mortuary chamber. The mound of the second building was about three times as long as the oval barrow of the first and was probably put up soon afterwards. Like West Kennett, Wayland's Smithy has now been restored (left, bottom left).

Excavations in the 1950s and 1960s established that in many cases a wooden structure had stood on the site before the barrow was built and had housed bodies over a long period of time. The great long barrow of Fussell's Lodge in Wiltshire revealed just such a wooden collective grave containing four clear groups of disarticulated bones. These represented from 53 to 57 bodies which had been placed there at intervals over many generations. It had eventually been allowed to decay and collapse and, after a fire had been lit on the site, the bodies had been buried under the long mound. The wooden structure was dated to the beginning of the fourth millennium BC by radiocarbon but the barrow itself must have been built some time after this.

The long cairn at Lochhill in Kirkcudbrightshire, excavated in 1969 and 1970, also revealed a wooden structure buried under the stones of the mound. This one, however, had a curved facade, a wooden version of the stone 'horns' of the chambered cairns of western Scotland; the sepulchre was a stone-lined trench. It too gave a radiocarbon date at the beginning of the fourth millennium BC. After this structure had been burned, presumably deliberately, the long stone chambered cairn was piled over its remains. A curved stone facade was built just in front of where the wooden one had been and a short megalithic chamber was set up in line with, and just in front of, the earlier trench grave.

It is clear that the idea of adding long mounds or cairns to earlier wooden collective tombs was widespread and was not necessarily part of the earliest ritual of the collective burial people: it could have been adopted by them at a later stage. These wooden collective tombs resemble the passage graves only in terms of burial rite.

The cairns in south-west England

Scattered through several counties on both sides of the Severn estuary is a compact group of about 170 chambered cairns, with a few outliers as far east as Wiltshire and as far north as north Wales. The majority of the sites cluster round the estuary itself and this fact gave rise to the belief that the builders had arrived by sea. The general form of the cairns is long and trapeze- or wedge-shaped, the wider end having horn-like projections. The inner faces of these horns are, however, usually convex, not concave like those of the long cairns of the north. Many of the sites are 'transepted gallery graves', having a straight megalithic gallery with square side-chambers on both sides, opening on to the centre of the wider end. But there are a variety of other arrangements of chambers and some of the cairns have clearly gone through more than one phase of development. Unfortunately none of these possibly multi-period cairns has yet been investigated in the modern manner.

The burial ritual in the graves is again the collective one, and the bodies are not cremated. The number of individuals in a cairn varies from 3 or 4 to 48. The four side-chambers in the West Kennet long barrow in Wiltshire had been deliberately filled with chalk and soil. Under this fill were many bones, a few lying as articulated skeletons (the latest burials) but most being stacked in rows and piles, evidently after the bodies had completely decayed.

The sequence of cairn development may be well seen at Ty Isaf in Brecknockshire. The first building there was fairly clearly a form of cruciform passage grave under a small cairn, although there seems to be a great reluctance among specialists in this field to apply the term passage grave, with all its international implications, to small, round cairns with a central chamber and a passage! Later this small cairn was incorporated into a wedge-shaped, horned long cairn in which three other chambers were built, two of them entered from the long sides. A 'blind entrance' between the horns simulates the entrance to the transepted gallery in other similar cairns but here at Ty Isaf there is nothing behind it except solid cairn rubble. Here again there is a strong suggestion that the earliest collective tombs in the area were quite different from the majority and that the tradition of long mounds was brought in later and grafted on to these earlier megaliths.

At Wayland's Smithy in Berkshire a primary oval barrow, built of chalk on a base of sarsen boulders and about 16·5 metres long, covered a rectangular mortuary structure. This consisted of a pavement of sarsen slabs which was probably covered by a timber chamber which had eventually collapsed under the weight of the mound above. The remains of 12 or 14 adults and one child were found in this and the bones showed that they had obviously been dead for widely different lengths of time when finally interred.

A second enormous mound, trapeze shaped and about 55 metres long, was later added on top of the first and fitted with a transepted megalithic chamber at the southern, wider end. A burnt branch was found which seemed to represent a clearance of the ground just before the second barrow was built and gave a radiocarbon date of about 3600 BC. The first barrow is not thought to have been constructed more than a few decades before this.

If the first cairn at Ty Isaf was a type of small cruciform passage grave the curious transepted galleries in the Severn-Cotswold cairns—a feature not known elsewhere in Britain—may have been derived from this form of passage grave in a unique mingling of traditions (and people) after the long-cairn builders arrived.

The Clyde cairns

The second group of long chambered cairns in Britain lies around the estuary of the river Clyde in south-west Scotland. The cairns are similar to the Severn-Cotswold group: they tend to be rectangular or wedge-shaped with the wider end built concave to form a forecourt flanked by the horns of a curved facade. In the centre of this facade is the entrance to the tomb, a long megalithic lintelled gallery without transepts but usually split into several compartments by cross slabs. None of these cairns have yet been found to have been built in stages so the earlier forms are hypothetical.

Unfortunately only two Clyde cairns have so far been dated by radiocarbon. The Monamore site on the Isle of Arran has already been described. The Glenvoidean multi-period cairn on Bute has been dated to about the mid-third millennium BC. Now that the wooden horned structure at Lochhill in Kirkcudbright has been given a similar fourth-millennium date there is little reason to doubt the date from Monamore and it may be assumed that the horned cairns were being built around the Clyde—and doubtless in Ulster also, as well as in the Severn-Cotswold area—at around 4000 BC.

About half the burials found in the excavated Clyde tombs had been cremated and half were inhumation burials. The pottery and artefacts put in with the burials are mainly of early Neolithic type and several characteristic local varieties of the usual round-based pots appear.

One close study of the Clyde cairns has suggested that they evolved, in part at least, from simple earlier massive megalithic chambers, set within a round or an oval cairn, known as protomegaliths. This seems entirely reasonable and, if correct, would show yet again how the idea of the long horned cairn was planted on top of an earlier local tradition.

Passage graves in south-west Scotland

The passage graves of Britain are heavily concentrated in the far west and north of Scotland with only a scatter in other regions. The large numbers of horned long cairns in other territories does suggest that the builders of passage graves found such regions already occupied by megalith builders, and had to make do with the far north yet, on the other hand, simple passage graves may have been built at a very early stage in South Wales and the same phenomenon is seen in Dumfries-shire.

A striking feature of these tombs—and of some of the Scottish long cairns—is the relative frequency with which cremated human remains have been found in them. In England, by contrast, and in all other parts of the megalith builders' province, inhumation burial in the collective tombs seems to be the universal rite. This probably means that there was a well-established local Neolithic funerary tradition in Scotland which the megalith builders often adopted. On the other hand it may reflect the influence of the universal Irish tradition of cremation in collective tombs.

Bargrennan, giving its name to the small group of passage graves in south-west Scotland, was excavated in 1949 and proved already to have been disturbed and emptied. The round cairn is about 13·7 metres in diameter and a simple, wedge-shaped megalithic passage enters from the south side. The central chamber is rectangular and is hardly differentiated from the passage; the whole thing was roofed with massive stone lintels resting on heavy drystone walling mounted on the orthostats below. The passage ended 2·4 metres from the edge of the cairn and may therefore have been deliberately blocked at the end of the tomb's use.

Although the chamber, over which two capstones were still in position, had been robbed, the outer part of the passage was found to be undisturbed, buried under its dislodged capstones and under rubble fallen from the cairn. Here was found a paved floor on which was a layer of stones and dark soil up to 46 centimetres thick but containing no finds. A clay-lined pit appeared on the north side of the passage with signs of burning and in it was a deposit of black soil and fragments of burnt bone. The finds made were not helpful for dating and the age of this and the few other south-west Scottish passage graves is a matter for conjecture.

Of considerable interest for passage grave origins are the excavations of two cairns at Mid Gleniron farm in Wigtownshire by the late Dr. John Corcoran from 1963 to 1965. The first phase at Mid Gleniron 1 proved originally to have consisted of two separate small round cairns looking remarkably like simple passage graves. Since both were only 6·1 metres in diameter and about 3 metres apart, and since the simple rectangular chambers of both faced just north of east, it seems that the southerly one was built first.

Later, both round mounds were incorporated in a single horned long cairn, the chamber of the northern one being slightly elongated and converted into one opening between the horns; the chamber of the southern cairn seems to have been sealed by the added rubble. A third megalithic chamber was added at this time between the two round cairns and opened on to the west side of the new long cairn. The forecourt of the new structure was the focus of ceremonies presumably connected with the burial of the dead. A few fragments of pottery and many pieces of charcoal were found on its floor and the whole forecourt was eventually blocked with a mass of rubble, a carefully built wall sealing the entrance to the tomb itself. All three chambers had been cleared out a hundred years or more earlier so no information was forthcoming about the primary burials. However, a number of cremation burials were inserted into the body of the cairn at a later date and four Bronze Age cinerary urns were found with these. The earlier finds were not informative and no absolute dates of any kind are available for the site.

The second cairn at Mid Gleniron was similar to the first but here a single small passage grave had been buried inside a horned long chambered cairn so that the passage of the former opened on to the south long side of the latter.

The excavations at Mid Gleniron marked a turning point in our understanding not only of the evolution of the megalithic tombs of Britain but also of their full significance in these islands. This type of evidence—of a physical succession of different kinds of structures—is the only one which provides any firm ground for the typological speculations which have been the mainstay of past studies of chambered tombs. There is clear evidence at Mid Gleniron that the earliest tombs in the region were of a kind which would be described as undifferentiated passage graves elsewhere, the same kind of monument that antedated the great cruciform passage grave of Knowth in the Boyne valley. The larger Bargrennan passage graves can reasonably be regarded as a development from these small ones, presumably before the fashion for horned long cairns became dominant. Because the study of Scottish chambered tombs often proceeds in isolation, these early cairns do not seem to have been compared with passage graves before now. In fact the term seems almost to have been avoided and with it also the local implications of the international distribution of these buildings.

The entrance to a side-chamber and the block of stone that plugged it, and the tall facing slab for a corner buttress at Maes Howe — the last being a feature unique to this extraordinarily finely built passage grave in Orkney. The local sandstone splits absolutely regularly into slabs ideal for drystone building.

The central chambers of one group of passage graves in north Scotland and Orkney were divided by projecting slabs into 'stalls'. This was the plan at Camster Round (above) although the chamber there remained small enough to lie under a round cairn. With increased numbers of stalls, however, chamber and mound grew longer and at Unstan (left) the mound was twice enlarged. Unstan is unusual for having one side-chamber (below) as well as stalls. A drystone barrel-vault may have roofed the tomb.

Passage graves in the Highlands and Islands

The distribution of passage graves throughout the rest of Scotland is clearly maritime; they are found on the Hebridean islands, in the northern counties of Caithness and Sutherland and in the Orkney and Shetland Isles. This pattern complements the maritime distribution of the Breton, Irish, Welsh and south-west Scottish passage graves and suggests that the idea of these tombs was carried along the western seaways.

Fieldwork and excavation in the northern parts of Scotland has shown that, as in the south-west, small passage graves were there at an early date but were succeeded by much larger horned long cairns. The progression has long been clear in Shetland where 'heel-shaped cairns' were at first simple round passage graves, perhaps 9 metres in diameter, and sometimes, as at Vementry, with a cruciform chamber which then had masonry added to them to convert them into short horned cairns with a characteristic heel-like plan. At Vementry the horned cairn was in the form of a lower platform of masonry built around the small passage grave and blocking its entrance. Others, presumably slightly larger, lack the primary passage grave and have the chamber opening between the horns in the manner normal in long cairns. If cruciform passage graves are a secondary development in Britain one might suppose that those in Shetland arrived there some time later than in the rest of the country.

The cairn at Tulach an t'Sionnaich by Loch Calder in Caithness also proved to have been built in distinct stages. Here, however, two alterations had been made to the monument. The primary cairn was a round passage grave about 10.7 metres in diameter and with a simple chamber: this was later surrounded by a lower platform—a heel-shaped cairn—which blocked the entrance. Both these structures faced more or less due south. Later still an enormous horned long cairn 59·4 metres in length was built around the heel-shaped one and its long axis was tilted clockwise about 15° from those of the first two. Bones of two young adults were found in the cairn, together with fragments of an elderly person and a child, but little else. Again no radiocarbon dates are available and there is no clue to the age of the first simple passage grave on the site except that it is now known that some horned long cairns could have been built as early as 4000 BC.

In Orkney and Caithness are the most spectacular and individual examples of the development of passage grave architecture, culminating in Maes Howe—a monument of an architectural sophistication that can hold its own with anything in contemporary Malta or Iberia. The reasons for these remarkable northern developments must be partly social and partly environmental. Orkney and Caithness are composed of Old Red sandstone which splits into huge slabs or flags, ideal for drystone architecture. The availability of such building material, often in the form of very large stone 'planks', seems to have led to dramatic architectural developments in several periods of prehistory.

There are simple, small passage graves in the Orkney Isles and in Caithness and these prove to be early in the megalithic sequence judging by

Tulach an t'Sionnaich and Mid Gleniron. Camster Long, in Caithness, seems to have two small passage graves entombed inside an enormous long cairn, this time with horns at both ends. Two types of passage grave can be seen, each of which evidently gave rise to a highly distinctive line of development. In the first place there are small cairns like Huntersquoy, Bigland Round and Knowe of Craie, all on Orkney, in which the central chamber is divided into compartments or stalls by huge upright slabs projecting from the wall. These cairns were gradually built larger and longer, particularly on Rousay island, so that the chamber—still reached by a short passage—became a long gallery with a number of stalls formed by the many projecting slabs. The Knowe of Yarso has a chamber 7·6 metres long divided into four pairs of compartments, the whole being inside a rectangular cairn with rounded corners and nearly 15 metres in length. Unstan is similar and in this case the round cairn seems to have been enlarged twice. This cairn produced many of the characteristic Unstan bowls—round-based vessels decorated with incised geometric designs—as well as the more ordinary early Neolithic plain, bag-shaped pottery and leaf-shaped flint points of the same period. Fragments of human skeletons were found in each compartment.

These stalled cairns, as they are known, reached their finest development in structures like Midhowe and Blackhammer on Rousay island. The former is a rectangular cairn measuring 32·6 by 14·5 metres, with an entrance in the south-east end. This leads to an enormous, dry-walled, stalled gallery 23·2 metres long and up to 2·4 metres wide, divided into twelve opposing pairs of compartments by huge, upright, sandstone slabs projecting from the walls. The remains of 25 individuals were found in the chamber, as well as an Unstan bowl and two plain vessels.

The great length of these chambers means that a 'beehive' corbelled stone roof was not possible and the projecting slabs presumably also served to support a roof of another kind. This might have been flat and made of overlapping stone lintels but there are no reports of stone slabs being found inside the collapsed chambers. Instead these were found full of stones and there is a clear possibility that the Neolithic architects on Orkney had mastered the technique of building the barrel-vault and that long, tunnel-like drystone roofs covered the stalled cairns. If so they would have been by far the most advanced stone buildings in Europe in the fourth and third millennia BC.

The second and less common type of small passage grave is cruciform in plan: the two small cairns on the Calf of Eday island are good examples as is that on Wideford Hill on mainland Orkney (the latter, round cairn has been twice enlarged). These simple passage graves with side-chambers gave rise to more complex forms. In the first place, the chamber was occasionally elongated laterally, into a gallery like that of a stalled cairn but with large numbers of side-chambers instead of the stalls. The most spectacular example of this development is the Holm of Papa Westray, a huge long cairn on a tiny island of that name which can never have supported a community

The false entrance and horned forecourt of Belas Knap, a long ▶
chambered cairn in the Severn/Cotswold region.

large enough to be capable of building such a massive temple-tomb. The cairn is 35 metres long and about 17 metres wide and the entrance was from the middle of the south-east long side. This leads to the central dry-walled gallery about 20 metres long and 1·5 metres wide and running along the long axis of the mound. Ten small, low doors from the sides of this gallery and two more from the ends lead to 14 small corbelled side-chambers (two being double ones).

The other direction taken by the evolving cruciform passage graves was towards greater size and sophistication, and this line culminated in Maes Howe. The cairns remain round but they achieve a diameter of up to 24 metres (Quanterness) or even 35 metres (Maes Howe itself). At Quoyness six irregularly planned, low side-chambers open off the high central chamber but at Quanterness—recently excavated by Professor Colin Renfrew —there are six beautifully rectangular side-chambers which open from an equally symmetrical central one. In both these buildings the roofing of the central chamber is extremely sophisticated: the long side walls rise vertically for several feet and then lean inwards like an inverted V until they approach close enough to be capped with flat lintels. The chamber at Quanterness is intact and about 3·5 metres high but that at Quoyness has lintels 4 metres above the floor. The roofs are exactly the same design as the those devised perhaps 3,000 years later by the ancient Maya of Central America to roof their stone palaces and temples—an intriguing example of the independent invention of the same device to solve a similar problem. These roofs stand high among the many remarkable creations of Neolithic architects in the Orkneys.

Several examples of human bones found inside Quanterness have been carbon-dated. The earliest of these seems to have been interred in the late fourth millennium BC and the latest in the mid-third, at the same time that the main occupation of Skara Brae was taking place.

Maes Howe is much better known and has more unusual architectural features but overall it is of a similar standard of workmanship and design as Quanterness and Quoyness. The great round mound stands within an encircling ditch. The earliest radiocarbon dates given by the peat from the base of the ditch were equivalent to about 2800, 2500 and 2200 BC. This passage grave is therefore presumably as old as, or older than, the average of these dates and may have been built in the first half of the third millennium BC.

The total length of the passage is at least 16·3 metres but most of the outermost 6·9 metres may never have been roofed. The outer part of this section is dry-walled but the innermost 7 metres on both sides consists of two enormous stone slabs on edge which run the full length and are 1·32 metres wide. They thus stand not much less in height than the roof of the passage which is here formed of a third similar enormous slab. These great stones must weigh at least three metric tonnes each and probably more.

The central chamber is 4·6 metres square but each corner consists of a projecting buttress of solid masonry. These support the corbelled roof which

◀ *The long gallery of the chambered cairn of West Kennett in southern England.*

must once have risen 4·6 metres above the floor. Most of the stones forming the walls and roof are huge megalithic slabs and span nearly the whole width of the chamber. Three small side chambers open from the main room, one in each inner wall. The roof of each of these is formed of a single flat slab and the floors are above the level of the floor of the main chamber. The narrow entrances were evidently each closed by one of the stone blocks which were found still lying on the floor of the main chamber.

Maes Howe and Quanterness have been dated to the late fourth and first half of the third millennia BC by radiocarbon and several of the stalled cairns on Orkney have recently been put into the same time span in the same way. However, they still pose the same basic problems as the megaliths of Atlantic Europe. Were they primarily tombs or did they also serve as temples? Does the magnificent architecture—which was clearly developed locally in these northern islands—reflect only the ideal building material or were special kinds of people needed to sieze the opportunities thus offered? Were these remarkable buildings communal structures of some kind or do they imply a professional priesthood?

As far as the architecture of the Orkney-Cromarty buildings is concerned there can surely be little doubt that professional engineers were involved in their design and construction. At Maes Howe for example the numerous small instances of high standards inevitably seem to point to this conclusion. The huge slabs are accurately levelled and plumbed, neat underpinning of small stones being used to achieve this. The corners of the slabs have often been rebated to fit their neighbours and the huge blocks have obviously been chosen and fitted together with immense care. The steady improvement in the design and construction of the various groups of tombs also implies that a class of professional builders was accumulating knowledge and skill over many generations and it could be inferred also that another professional class existed for whom this work was being done and which provided the motive for it and the wealth to pay for it. To regard these buildings only as tombs because skeletons have been found in most of them would be naive. When newly built these great cairns would have shown neatly built, stone-walled faces to the world—not the featureless green mounds of today—and must be regarded as proper roofed buildings. In the absence of cement and mortar there was probably no other way to build a free-standing structure with a stone roof and the Orkney cairns undoubtedly represent one of the greatest architectural achievements that Neolithic Europe can offer. The huge roofed chambers must have been as amazing to the contemporary Neolithic peasants—and as satisfying to their builders— as were the great Norman and Gothic cathedrals and as are today's Apollo spacecraft to the respective spectators and creators of such technological achievements.

The finds which have been made over the years in the chambered mounds of the far north include the kind of early Neolithic pottery that such sites have yielded everywhere in Britain. In spite of regional variations in the round-based pottery bowls, the material culture of the whole of Britain at that time is remarkably uniform and does not by itself provide many clues as to whether the society of the time was divided into distinct classes or not.

Who were the tombs for?

Because the archaeology of early Neolithic Britain consists mainly of funerary monuments—the collective tombs and their contents—it is impossible to construct a complete archaeological picture of the material culture of the society of the time. However there are a few clues as to whether the tombs were the sepulchres of the whole of the rural Neolithic population or whether, on the other hand, they were the monuments and memorials of a special élite group of some kind.

The complete dominance of impressive, monumental collective graves in Neolithic times might well suggest—were there no Continental and Mediterranean evidence to the contrary—that this was the standard method of interment for the whole population at that time. Yet even if judgement is suspended for the moment on the relevance of the foreign evidence, there are clear signs from Britain itself that this was not the case, and that the people put into the great mounds and cairns were a small and select group of the population. In 1954 Professor Stuart Piggott reviewed the admittedly meagre evidence for other kinds of burial in the Neolithic period. Several examples of single graves were known then, notably skeletons found in the ditches of the causewayed camps at Windmill Hill in Wiltshire and Whitehawk in Sussex. These seemed to be fairly casual interments without any surface markers over the graves. Of special interest too are the few graves found at Neolithic flint mines such as Cissbury and Blackpatch in Sussex. At Cissbury, for example, a young man was found buried in the infill of one of the mine-shafts while at Blackpatch two round barrows were found which had actually been built over filled-in shafts. In one of these were two crouched skeletons with a cremation scattered over the bones of both: there was no suggestion that the tomb marked anything other than a single funeral for three people. In the other barrow was one skeleton. The beginning of mining activity at Cissbury has been dated by radiocarbon to about 3300 BC and that at Blackpatch was under way by 3900 BC.

Primary evidence about the nature of the megalith builders comes from the abundant preserved skeletal material. T. H. Bryce, Professor of Anatomy at the University of Glasgow in the early decades of this century, explored a number of Neolithic and Bronze Age cairns on Arran and Bute, recovering several skulls of both periods in the process. In general the Neolithic skulls were long-headed, or *dolichocephalic*, with the proportion of the width to the length of the braincase being relatively low at less than 75 % (a cephalic index of less than 75 %). This contrasted with many of the skulls found in Early Bronze Age short cists which tended to be short-headed or *brachycephalic*, with cephalic indices of 80 % or more. Though Bryce's Neolithic skulls in fact varied quite widely in the dolichocephalic range they were also distinct from the Early Bronze Age skulls in a number of other anatomical features while resembling the skulls found in the English

Neolithic long barrows very closely. Bryce considered that the two groups were of the same race and agreed with other authorities of the time that the general British Neolithic ethnic type was a northern branch of a specific prehistoric Mediterranean race of long-headed people of short stature. These people seem to have been concentrated in Atlantic and northern Europe in Neolithic times and are found in the collective and megalithic tombs of the period. The suggestion was made then that the centre of the dispersion of the race was north Africa—hence the name 'Eurafrican' for this type.

In 1926 G. M. Morant published data on 144 Neolithic skulls from long barrows. He concluded that there was every reason to believe that these were of essentially the same racial type as the Scottish Neolithic skulls. For example the average cephalic index of the long-barrow skulls was found to be 71·7 while that of the Scottish skulls was 72·7. It is also worth mentioning that Morant's study of the later Early Bronze Age skulls showed that these were not so racially homogeneous as the Neolithic ones and gave clear evidence of hybridization between the immigrant Beaker people and the people descended from the earlier Neolithic population.

The significance of the racial homogeneity of the Neolithic skulls of England and Scotland must obviously depend on what social status one thinks was enjoyed by the people collectively buried in the long barrows and chambered mounds. It would mean one thing if they were members of the whole community and something different if they were members of a separate sect. If Darlington's view is correct that the megalith builders were a stable caste—presumably genetically related and intermarrying on a nationwide scale like the old European aristocracies—the close similarity of the skulls would be easily explained, as would intermarrying between them and the dominant Beaker people who came soon after 2500 BC. It is unfortunate that there is not available an equivalent set of skulls which can be confidently said to have belonged to the Neolithic peasant class.

The survival in peripheral parts of Britain of the genes of a Mediterranean people from Neolithic times has long been known. The much greater frequency of dark hair in Wales and Ireland as well as detailed studies of other physical characteristics of the modern Welsh and Irish support this view. More recently Dr. J. R. Baker has pointed out that there is new evidence from distributions of blood groups which gives this hypothesis further support. In north-west Wales and south-west Ireland the frequencies of the O and A blood groups are unusually high and low respectively by the general standards of the modern British and Irish populations. The A blood group gene also still has a similar low frequency in many Mediterranean lands such as North Africa, Corsica, Sardinia, Sicily and the southern half of Italy. Likewise the O group gene is unusually frequent in some of these same territories, especially Corsica and Sardinia. Whatever the explanation there can be very little doubt that elements in the British and Irish Neolithic populations were derived from a Mediterranean stock.

Chapter VII Temples and Observatories

On a low hill near Callanish farm, on the north shore of Loch Roag—an arm of the sea on the western side of the Isle of Lewis in the Outer Hebrides—there stands a remarkable formation of very tall and thin standing stones. They are laid out in the form of a cross and are visible from many directions as a row of blunt spikes on the skyline. At dusk after a fine summer evening in 1934 Alexander Thom, then Professor of Engineering at the University of Oxford, was sailing his boat into Loch Roag to find an anchorage for the night. The full moon was just rising in the east and, as it came up over the nearby low hills, the standing stones were starkly silhouetted against its yellow disc. It must have been a striking sight and from that moment Professor Thom's interest in these strange prehistoric megaliths was kindled, to be followed up by more than forty years of painstaking fieldwork and measurement throughout the length and breadth of Britain.

Stone circles and henges

In late Neolithic and Chalcolithic times—a period of seven or eight centuries which is now known to have started at around 2500 BC—a characteristic type of monument was built in large numbers all over the stonier regions of Britain and Ireland and Brittany. Great boulders and slabs of rock were laboriously dragged to selected sites and levered upright, singly and in formations, into sockets prepared for them. Most of the stones were grouped in circles or near-circles, but many stand isolated or in groups of two or three. The nature of these sites is such that it is extraordinarily difficult to find out anything definite about them by the traditional archaeological methods of surveying and excavation. In early and middle Neolithic times similar megalithic slabs were commonly built into chambers which were buried under large mounds and used as sepulchres for the dead; in such cases objects were put into the chambers with the bodies and have been preserved so that a good estimate can be made of their date and purpose. With standing stones, however, such direct associations between megaliths and archaeological objects are extremely rare; the pillars stand alone, mute and mysterious, and it is scarcely surprising that more myths and fantasies have grown up around them than about almost any other prehistoric remains.

It was the sight of the standing stones of Callanish on the skyline one summer evening in 1934 that set Alexander Thom, then Professor of Engineering at Oxford, off on his survey of all the standing stones of the late Neolithic period in Britain and Brittany. It is Professor Thom who has now confirmed the possible astronomical significance of so many of them.

When the stones stand in a ring, graves are often found in the space so enclosed, usually near the centre; these frequently yield Early Bronze Age pottery and other objects. But such graves do not automatically reveal that the primary purpose of the stone circle was a graveyard although they do suggest that it must be at least as old as the buried objects concerned, perhaps a little older. The burials might have been added some time after the ring had been put up. Even graves are lacking at the isolated standing stones, most of which have consequently to be dated simply by assuming that they are of the same period as the circles.

From a careful analysis by H. A. W. Burl of the kind of pottery found on the circle sites it is clear that, while the earliest of these were probably built in middle Neolithic times—perhaps around 3000 BC—the majority seem to have been erected and used in the late Neolithic/Chalcolithic period and in the Early Bronze Age, say from about 2500 to 1500 BC. This is borne out by the few reliable radiocarbon dates available for these sites, most of which fall between about 2300 and 1200 bc. It is thus clear that the standing stones represent a second great phase of megalith building, quite distinct from the early and middle Neolithic collective tombs of the first phase both in time and function. Indeed the only link between the two megalithic phases seems at first sight to be the use of the great stones themselves.

Henge monuments consist of circular or near-circular areas, defined and enclosed by a ditch and, usually, by an *outer* bank. They are thus clearly not defence works, the banks of which would have been inside the ditches. Whereas the stone circles are found, again for obvious reasons, mainly in large numbers in rocky and highland areas the henge monuments are most numerous in the lowland areas of the south-east and central parts of the country where ditches are easier to dig in the deeper soil. Enough henge sites contain stone circles to make it plain that the two kinds of buildings are closely related. Indeed one might argue that all these circular sites should be grouped together as circular ritual places and that some lack stone circles because of the lack of suitable boulders nearby and that others lack a surrounding ditch and bank because of the hardness of the underlying rock in the highland areas.

Professor Thom has shown that many of the groups of standing stones in the British Isles are circular but that the stones of others often lie very closely to accurately drawn ellipses. Still others seem to have been built around flattened circles and egg shapes, their perimeters always apparently being constructed systematically out of arcs of circles whose radii are in multiples of megalithic yards. In the case of the egg-shaped sites the wider end is usually a half circle while the narrower end is formed of arcs of larger circles drawn from the corners of an isosceles triangle the sides of which are also normally in whole numbers of megalithic yards. The flattened circles are likewise based on a true circle, with the flattened part made of an arc of a much larger circle.

It should be explained at this point that such geometrical constructions for stone circles are drawn in units of length of 2 feet 8·64 inches or 0·829 metres. This prehistoric 'short yard', known as the megalithic yard, was discovered mathematically by Professor Thom by analysing the dimensions of a large number of stone rings which are true circles and which he had himself accurately planned. Units of a megalithic yard emerged in this way in scores of sites as did a multiple of $2\frac{1}{2}$ such yards known as the megalithic rod; this is equal to 6·8 feet or 2·073 metres. It is remarkable how often non-circular stone rings will fit a simple geometrical pattern drawn in megalithic yards, Avebury providing one of the more spectacular and impressive examples.

The discovery that elaborate geometrical knowledge—previously thought to have been unknown before the time of the ancient Greeks perhaps 2,000 years later—and advanced skills in planning and field measurement underlie the design of the stone circles is surely one of the great breakthroughs in British archaeology this century. It has revealed a totally unexpected aspect of what appears at first sight to be a barren and unpromising group of prehistoric structures. One conclusion could be that, since the megalithic yard and the geometry are found throughout Britain (and in Brittany as well), there was a class of wise men in existence at that time whose members designed temples and sanctuaries for their own purposes. This evidence could also suggest that such a class was a highly trained national one rather than formed of scattered bands of primitive shamans and medicine men. If this conclusion were favoured, the question would immediately arise where such a class could have been trained, and one answer would surely have to be—somewhere among one of the main centres of the Neolithic population where the finest of these monuments are located.

A sophisticated geometrical shape is not the only quality to have been revealed in the stone circles. Scores of them, as well as many isolated standing stones, have been carefully measured in relation to their visible horizons and it has been found that a large number could have had a practical astronomical function, so many in fact that there cannot be much doubt that the designers of these sites all over the country were highly competent astronomers.

Before the invention of accurate, small observing instruments—only a few hundred years ago—the only way that the position of the sun, moon, planets or stars could be precisely marked and measured was by noting the positions where they rose and set on the horizon. With this method, if the observer chooses his position carefully and adjusts it rapidly sideways as the celestial body goes down, he can exactly mark its setting at some conspicuous natural feature on the horizon—a V-shaped notch or a prominent mountain peak. Two standing stones pointing to the notch—or a single flat-sided one orientated towards it—will serve both to mark the observer's position permanently and also to show where the horizon mark is. The line from the stone (the backsight) to the horizon mark (the foresight) is known as the *alignment*.

This technique can easily be used to pinpoint the rising and setting positions of the fixed stars, which change extremely slowly over centuries,

North Sea

Circles ⠄⠆⠇

Alignments ×ˣ×

0   750 kms

Stone circles and alignments of the 3rd and early 2nd millennia BC in Britain, Ireland and Brittany.

The standing stones of Britain, Brittany and Ireland appear to have had no connection with burial rites when they were first put up, and recent radiocarbon dates have shown that most of them are as distinct from the megalithic collective tombs in time as they are in function. At first sight it is only the use of the great stones themselves that links the two phases of megalith building. Many of the groups of stones form circles, like the outer ring at Stonehenge (top and bottom left), the Rollright Stones (top right) or Castlerigg, where the circle is flattened, (bottom right); others lie very closely to accurately drawn ellipses, like the inner group at Stonehenge (top left).

but it can also be used to track and understand the movements of the sun and moon, which change their rising and setting positions relatively quickly over fixed cycles. In this way it would theoretically be possible to work out the exact number of days in the year and thus to construct an accurate calendar. The sun is most important from a calendric point of view if regularity and accuracy are desired. The moon's movements, on the other hand, are much more complicated but, if understood, can give a vital clue to the prediction of eclipses, an ability which would surely confer immense prestige on any religious leader or prophet.

Because of the tilt on the earth's axis, the rising and setting positions of the sun fluctuate throughout each year on either side of due east and west respectively. The size of the arc of the horizon across which these positions move varies according to the latitude of the observer: at the equator it is nearly 47° (twice the angle of tilt of the axis, now 23° 27′). At the latitude of central Scotland, about 55° north, the swing is about 90°, while at the Arctic Circle the rising and setting points run round the entire 360° of the horizon. Thus at the latitude of Argyllshire—where some of the most important standing stone 'observatories' are situated—the midwinter sun sets in the south-west but six months later the sunset postion has moved right round to the north-west (the corresponding sunrise positions are in the south-east and north-east). If it were possible to pinpoint the day when sunset occurred at its furthest north (or south), the day of midsummer (or midwinter) would be exactly defined and the length of the year precisely known.

Unfortunately it is not quite as simple as that. At the equinoxes (March 21st and September 21st, the dates on which the sun rises exactly in the east and sets in the west) the position of sunset changes quickly: everyone must have noticed how rapidly the days lengthen or shorten at this time of year. However, since the position of the sunset is moving steadily in one direction, not much use can be made of it at the equinoxes. At the solstices, however, when the sun is rising and setting at its extreme northerly or southerly position (June 21st and December 21st respectively), the rate of daily change is extremely small, far too little to be detected by casual observation. Yet it is essential to know the exact day of the solstice if the number of days in a year is to be known and an exact calendar constructed, so how is this to be achieved in a non-literate Neolithic society?

The answer is that even the minute change in the sun's real movement (not to be confused with its daily motion) during the 24 hours before and after the solstice—equivalent to about $\frac{1}{70}$ of the apparent diameter of the solar disc—can be detected if the line of sight to the horizon is long enough. If our imaginary Neolithic astronomer found a clear-cut mountain peak in about the right position and say 30 kilometres away, he could arrange his position so that, on each evening leading up to the solstice, he made the sun disappear behind the peak and its upper edge just flash into view again at the right slope as it slid down. If it was near midsummer he would find that his position had moved several feet to the *left* (south) on each successive evening, as the sunset position moved imperceptibly to the *right*. However

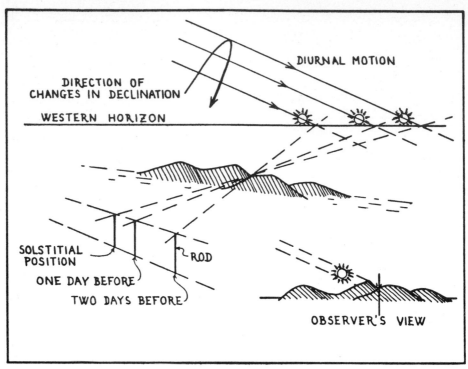

By marking a place from which the sun can be seen vanishing behind a fixed point on the horizon like a cleft in the hills, an observer may begin to time the movements of the sun and build up a calendar.

because the horizon marker was at a great distance even the last tiny movement of just under half a minute of arc along the horizon would be represented by a lateral movement of about 4 metres at the observer's position. Thereafter the 'minimum flash' positions—each of which should have been marked with a peg or stake—would start to move north again and our prehistoric astronomer would know that the solstice had passed. After two or three years of such successful observations he would feel confident enough to have a permanent marker—a tall standing stone—set up at the most southerly of these pegs. There the day of midsummer could be checked from the stone since only on the longest day of the year would the sun's edge momentarily re-appear at the base of the right slope of the chosen mountain as it slid down behind it.

Many standing stones and stone circles are situated so that they can be used as observing positions for watching the sun at the solstices and equinoxes, or the moon at the limits of its more complex cycles of movements across the sky. Far too many stones have been found with these qualities, and with some built-in indication of the direction in which to look for the horizon marker, for their astronomical siting to be dismissed as chance. The conclusion is that the leaders of late Neolithic/Chalcolithic society in Britain were intensely concerned with practical astronomy and had made considerable advances in it.

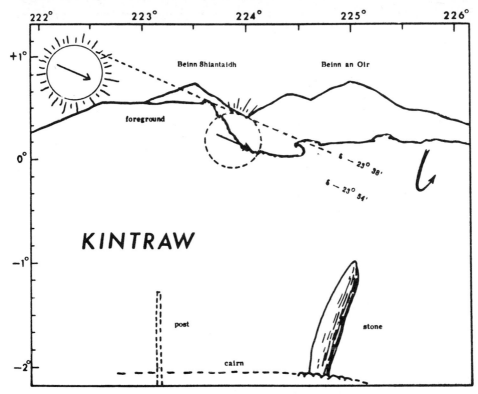

222°   223°   224°   225°   226°

+1°

Beinn Shiantaidh   Beinn an Oir

foreground

0°   δ – 23° 38'

δ – 23° 54'

KINTRAW

–1°

post   stone

–2°   cairn

At Kintraw a standing stone and an artificial platform recently found nearby with two conspicuous boulders at one end of it align with a point on the horizon between two mountain peaks where the sun would have set at the midwinter solstice at about 1800 BC.

Three solstice sites

On the west coast of the Kintyre peninsula, about 19 kilometres south of Tarbert, are the standing stones of Ballochroy. Three monoliths stand in a line pointing north-east/south-west and two of them are flat slabs with very smooth northern faces; these faces are exactly aligned on two peaks on the island of Jura clearly visible 29 kilometres away across the sea in the north-west. The front edges of the three stones together form a line which points at the west end of Cara island, 11 kilometres to the south-west. Thus there are three long alignments indicated by the Ballochroy stones themselves (in the opposite directions, north-east, and south-east, the horizon is close and featureless).

The west of Cara island marks the position of the setting sun at midwinter in about 1800 BC (with an astronomical position, or declination, of −23° 54′), while one of the indicated peaks on Jura gives the midsummer position for the same period (declination +23° 54′). The great distance away of the Jura peaks means that, given good weather and favourable atmospheric conditions, the days of midsummer could be exactly pinpointed with the apparatus at Ballochroy.

101

Sixty-five kilometres or so to the north is another standing stone near Kintraw farm from which a splendid view is to be had to the south-west down Loch Craignish. Jura is 45 kilometres away, and the sun setting in the conspicuous V-shaped notch between two of the most prominent peaks there would have had a declination of $-23° 54'$, suitable again for the midwinter solstice at about 1800 BC. Both Ballochroy and Kintraw are exceptionally important sites because of the great distance from them of the horizon marks, which are, at the southern site at least, clearly indicated by the stones themselves.

Preliminary observations at Kintraw to set up the exact position of the site could not have been done from the field beside the stone (from which Jura is nearly wholly obscured) but must have been carried out on slightly higher ground to see over the obstruction. The place had to be on a steep slope a short distance to the north-east, beyond a precipitous gorge containing a stream. Excavations in 1970 and 1971 on a more level terrace on this slope discovered an artificial platform of rubble, with a conspicuous observation point at one end of it, made from two massive boulders, at the exact spot predicted by the astronomical theory. This discovery has dramatically confirmed Professor Thom's diagnosis of the astronomical function of the Kintraw stones and, by implication, of many other similar sites also.

The Cultoon stone circle stands on the west coast of the island of Islay, Argyllshire, and was excavated in 1974 and 1975. No deductions or even guesses about its astronomical potential had previously been made, though an earlier survey by Professor Thom in 1973 had suggested that it was oval in shape. However, most of the stones were lying flat and no certainty about the exact original shape of the ring was possible. The excavation showed that the circle was unfinished; the 'fallen' stones had never in fact been set up at all. They were lying on the prehistoric ground surface where they had been abandoned, and up to 0·6 metres of peat had subsequently grown round them. Empty sockets for the stones were found, also buried under the peat, but they had become filled up with rubble and silt before the peat had formed.

Three stones were still standing and the positions of these, and of the many un-used sockets found, allowed the exact plan of the ring to be recovered. A computer revealed that the 16 positions fitted an ellipse with a long axis of 50 megalithic yards and a short one of 43·3 with only a few centimetres error all the way round. The point about the seemingly odd length of the short axis is that this particular ellipse has an eccentricity of one half: this means that the distance between its two foci is half the length of the long axis. An ellipse would be drawn on the ground with a loop of cord stretched tight round two pegs (the foci) and the cord here would have been 75 megalithic yards long. This neat geometrical construction could hardly have come about by chance.

It was clear that the long axis of this unfinished elliptical ring lay approximately north-east/south-west. On fine days at the site it became

The Ring of Brogar is surrounded by a ditch which, for its lack of any kind of complimentary bank, is obviously not defensive but which definitely sets apart the site of the stones. Mounds of earth around the enclosure appear to have some relationship with the moon's movements when aligned with points on the distant cliffs on the island of Hoy.

apparent that Ireland was quite clearly visible across the open sea to the south and south-west and a prominent mountain 88 kilometres away was almost exactly in the south-west. Careful measurements eventually revealed that, if the sun once set behind this mountain in the manner described (so that its upper edge just grazed the right slope), it would have had a declination of within a few minutes of $-23°\,54'$, the same prehistoric solstice position seen at many other sites. The 55-mile long alignment makes it one of the most accurate sun observatories known.

There can be little doubt that the Cultoon ring was positioned and designed very carefully in order to use a mountain in Ireland as a midwinter solstice sunset marker. Neither can there be much doubt that many, if not most, of the scores of other stone rings of Britain would, if carefully examined, also be found to be exactly positioned in relation to astronomically useful, distant features on the horizon. These discoveries— together with those concerning the geometry of the circles and the standardized system of measurement employed in setting them out—must completely transform our ideas about what late Neolithic society was like.

Another discovery made during the Cultoon excavations seems to throw light on the attitudes of the ordinary people to the standing stones. At the bases of the two standing monoliths on the site were found clusters of freshly struck flint flakes which, since they lay in the peat layer, must have been left there a long time after the circle was abandoned. There is little doubt that these caches of flints—which did not include any tools and seemed to be a flint knapper's debris—were deliberate offerings to the ancient stones by a superstitious Bronze Age peasantry.

The Clava cairns

At the north-eastern end of the Great Glen—a massive geological fault which splits the Scottish highlands diagonally in half—is a cluster of about 54 round chambered cairns known as the Clava cairns, some of which seem to be the closest thing to passage graves of the classic form which are to be found in the British Isles.

Certain features seem to favour a mid- or late third-millennium date for the cairns—the frequent occurrence, for example, of stone circles around them, the fact that some of them are true ring cairns without a passage and the fact that, while the sides of the central circular chambers in the better preserved structures do seem to show a slight inward tilt or overhang, there does not seem to have been enough debris in the excavated examples to accommodate a corbelled chamber inside a high mound. Finds are few and uninformative, however, and no radiocarbon dates are definitely attributable either to the construction of any of them or to any burials inside. The only clue comes from the cairn at Raigmore, Inverness-shire, where two radiocarbon dates of about 3000 to 2700 BC were obtained for charcoal from a pit close to the cairn and may approximately date the cairn itself. If this is so then the Clava cairns are perhaps unlikely to be early passage graves but must represent a later arrival of the tradition.

Hills behind the Ballinaby stone are markers for the moon's ▶
setting at its most northerly declination.

Two cairns at Balnuaran of Clava in Scotland are passage graves which, like New Grange in Ireland, are surrounded by a stone circle which is regularly geometrical in plan. In addition, both cairn passages are on the same line and when that is projected it meets the horizon at the point of the midwinter sunset some $3\frac{1}{2}$ to 4 thousand years ago. At Clava and New Grange there is thus a link between the people who built megalithic collective tombs and those astronomers who erected the stone circles.

◀ The stone at Kintraw and the distant Jura hills seen from the 'observation platform'.

Two of the three cairns at Balnuaran of Clava are passage graves and the middle one is a ring cairn with no entrance to the central chamber. Each is edged with a kerb of massive boulders and each has a stone circle surrounding it. Two of these are truly circular but the one on the north-east seems to be a geometrical egg shape. The central chambers are all very close to true circles—so that the massive blocks forming the base of the chamber walls must have been laid against a line drawn with a peg-and-cord 'compass'—but the diameters of these do not seem to be in units of megalithic yards.

There is no doubt, however, that the site was carefully planned as a single unit and laid out in relation to the prehistoric midwinter sunset in the south-west. Not only are the two cairn passages pointing in exactly the same direction (on a bearing of 225°) but they are on the same line. This line, if projected, meets the south-west horizon at the point of midwinter sunset some $3\frac{1}{2}$ to 4 thousand years ago. The Clava cairns thus closely resemble the great Boyne passage grave at New Grange which also has a stone circle around it and an entrance passage carefully arranged so that the rising sun at midwinter shone down it.

The Breton alignments

Probably the densest concentration of standing stones in north-west Europe is to be found in southern Brittany, in the Carnac area—that same zone which earlier in the Neolithic period saw the erection of many impressive chambered mounds, particularly passage graves. Single standing stones are found all over Brittany but at Carnac are rows of stones built on a scale which dwarfs anything in the British Isles.

On the basis of the few finds made, these alignments are generally assumed to belong to the same period as the British stone circles and standing stones. In recent years, however, an intensive campaign of surveying by Professor Thom and his family—which has been rightly described as one of the outstanding archaeological fieldwork projects of this century—has produced the first really accurate map of the stones and the first detailed explanations for their peculiar design and arrangement.

The great stone rows of Morbihan consist of three major alignments at Carnac and a fourth at Kerlescan. Each of the former group consists of several parallel rows of standing stones the heights of which tend to diminish consistently in one direction. The groups at Le Menec and Kermario run together for a distance of about 2·5 kilometres in a north-north-east direction with a gap of about 540 metres between them. Le Menec contains up to 12 rows with 1,099 stones still standing out of an original total of perhaps 1,500 or more; the lines occupy a strip of land up to 100 metres wide and run for 1,167 metres. The adjoining Kermario group now contains about 1,029 stones still standing, arranged in seven rows extending for at least 1,120 metres: the remains of another system of stone rows seem to be mingled with it. The Carnac system is separate and most impressive of all; nearly 3,000 stones still stand in rows running for nearly 4 kilometres.

When they are grouped, the standing stones of Brittany are mainly in lines rather than circles (right), with a great concentration of them in the south round Carnac (above). At Carnac itself nearly 3,000 stones run in parallel rows for almost 4 kilometres. The Breton alignments probably date, as the standing stones of Britain do, to the latter part of the megalith building period and are later than most of the collective tombs. They are set out according to precise geometrical principles but have not yet proved to have had any astronomical function.

Finds made at the Kermario stones include flints, an arrowhead, fragments of pottery and a polished axe but, although plenty of charoal and ash was found at the bases of the stones in early explorations, this was long before the days of radiocarbon dating. However, there is no real reason to doubt that the analogy with the British circles holds good and that the Breton rows date to a time later than many of the megalithic tombs— perhaps to the end of the third and the start of the second millennium BC.

The Thoms have shown that the great alignments were systematically set out according to elaborate geometrical principles in units of a standard length, commonly the megalithic rod. So far no practical tests—performable by archaeologists—have been devised to check whether the stones had any astronomical function, although the Thoms have identified standing stones nearby from which accurate observations of the moon could have been made. The most spectacular of these is the great monolith known as Le Grand Menhir Brisé, at Locmariaquer.

This colossal stone, now split into four pieces, must have weighed 355 metric tonnes or more when it was complete, and have stood at least 20 metres high. It could have served as a prominent foresight marker for the moon rising and setting at the four major extreme points of its 18·6 year cycle. The eight observing points which would have been needed to use the stone in this way—four for the rising and four for the setting of the moon— were identified around the Bay of Quiberon, one being right at the southern tip of the Quiberon peninsula to the south-west and some ten miles from the stone. At no less than four of these theoretical points prehistoric markers in the form of mounds or stones are still preserved. The inter-visibility of all the points and the site of the fallen monolith was checked at night with a light mounted on a water tower conveniently close by and found to be satisfactory. Thus the rising and setting of the moon when it was at its major and minor 'standstills' about 4,000 years ago would have been seen silhouetted far away against the great stone spike by an observer stationed at the appropriate one of the eight backsights.

The whole vast complex of alignments and standing stones in the Carnac region may thus have been designed as an integrated astronomical observatory. This, and the enormous scale of the engineering projects involved in building such Neolithic instruments, must suggest tremendous power and prestige. One wonders at the motives which impelled all the people concerned: they must surely have been derived from far more than a desire to carry out astronomical 'research' if they were to justify to the ordinary rural population the vast labour involved.

Chapter VIII Ceremonial Centres

Phase I at Stonehenge

On the chalk downs of southern England there were built in the second half of the third millennium BC several remarkable and large domestic sites which may well provide a rare clue to the nature of the society of the time. Here also stand two of the finest stone circles in Britain, Stonehenge and Avebury.

The unique character of Stonehenge among the standing stones of prehistoric Europe still presents a baffling puzzle. But new excavations there in the 1950s made it possible to sort out the complicated sequence of buildings and activities at the site and a number of radiocarbon dates have dated them with a fair degree of precision. The evolution of Stonehenge can now be tied in with the overall development of Neolithic society in southern England for which there is plenty of other evidence from the numerous burial mounds and other sites that have been excavated there over the years.

The first building at Stonehenge has been fairly well dated to the early third millennium BC by a radiocarbon measurement which was performed on one of the deer antler picks which were used to dig out its ditch and which were then tossed into it to be buried by silt. At this time the site consisted of a circular area about 105 metres across bounded by a bank and an outer ditch (the reverse of the usual arrangement at such henge sites), and with an entrance facing due north-east. The Heel stone stands 4·9 metres high a few metres outside the entrance and was perhaps put up at this time unless, as has also been suggested, it had been there for some time previously. There were probably two massive standing stones flanking the entrance.

A few feet within the bank a ring of 56 pits was dug into the chalk and almost immediately filled in again. The pits are known as the Aubrey holes after the seventeenth-century antiquary who noted them as shallow depressions still faintly visible in his day. Many of these pits were later used for cremation burials, probably over a long period of time, so their positions must always have been marked, perhaps by keeping them free of turf. The Aubrey holes were carefully planned: an exact circle 86·6 metres in diameter was drawn out on the ground, probably with a peg-and-cord compass, and the marks for the 56 holes were plotted round the ring at an average distance of 4·9 metres apart. It is also possible to place a perfect Pythagorean right-

Stonehenge (above) is the megalith builders' finest architectural endeavour and represents a vast fund of engineering and organizational skill. The midsummer sun rising over the Heel stone (below) would have impressed any audience inside the circle.

angled triangle—with sides of 40, 96 and 104 megalithic yards—over holes 56, 7 and 28 and over every other corresponding set.

There is a possibility that the Heel stone was set up as a calendar marker and that rows of wooden posts were set up nearby as marks for systematic observation of the moon. When the Heel stone is seen from the centre of Stonehenge it marks approximately the place on the north-east horizon where the midsummer sun rose in about 2900 BC: the sun rose to the left of the stone and a few minutes later would have stood over its tip (even now the actual first appearance of the orb is a little to the left of the stone). If it was a calendar stone it would not have been an accurate marker but may have been designed to create instead an impressive spectacle for the benefit of an audience—as indeed it still does. Much longer lines of sight would have been needed to serve as useful observing instruments.

The corrected date for the earliest Stonehenge, in the early third millennium BC, is much earlier than was thought even only a few years ago. It is not likely to be a coincidence that the huge chalk mound of Silbury Hill in north Wiltshire is about the same age. Prior to this time the earthworks which were set up by early and middle Neolithic society—long barrows, causewayed camps and some henges—involved in their construction a manpower which would not have been beyond the resources of a small, local rural community. Thanks to recent practical experiments with primitive equipment the amount of effort required to dig ditches and heap up mounds on the chalk downs of southern England is fairly accurately known, and an average long barrow could have been constructed—if one assumes a ten-hour working day—by a gang of about 100 men in about 24 days. Silbury Hill, however, is on a much vaster scale. A gang of 500 men would have had to have worked continuously for about 15 years to construct it and the logistical support for such a project would have been correspondingly large. This must have been more than a local project and clearly implies that a more centralized, organized society was coming into being on the chalklands of southern England by the time it was begun early in the third millennium BC.

Could the fact that Stonehenge I was built at the same time—probably as a combination of temple and astronomical observatory—mean that this new 'national' society was a theocratic one, ruled by priests or wise men? If so, these would have had to have had enough prestige to persuade the population to support a non-farming élite and to help in these huge building projects.

Avebury

The great circle at Avebury, 3 kilometres from Silbury Hill and some 24 kilometres north of Stonehenge, is another enormous engineering project in the henge tradition. Here the modern village stands partly within the huge prehistoric sanctuary, a circular area about 365 metres in diameter surrounded by a ditch almost 1·2 kilometres in length. This was 9 metres deep and 24 metres wide originally and outside it towers the huge bank, still

Massive sarsen stones still lie on the Marlborough Downs in southern England (left) whence 40 uprights and 35 lintels were dragged the 24 kilometres to Stonehenge (above) to build the final temple there in the late 3rd millennium BC. They were dressed to shape and, without any of the heavy machinery that is called for during restoration work at the site today (bottom left), levered into positions that precisely fitted a preordained, geometrical plan.

Apart from levers and rollers of timber and ropes of hide, most of the tools used in the building of Stonehenge would have been of the scale of the shoulderblade shovel and antler rake and pick found at contemporary flint mines (right). And with such tools even the biggest constructions of previous years, including the long barrows, would not have been beyond the resources of manpower of the local rural community. But with the same tools, Silbury Hill (above), which is near Stonehenge and contemporary with its first phase, would have involved five times the labour even to get it done within 15 years.

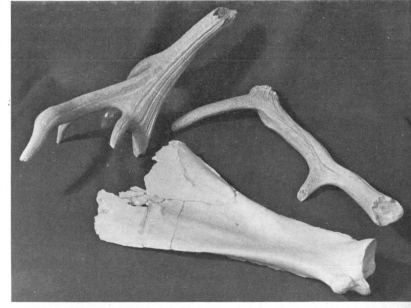

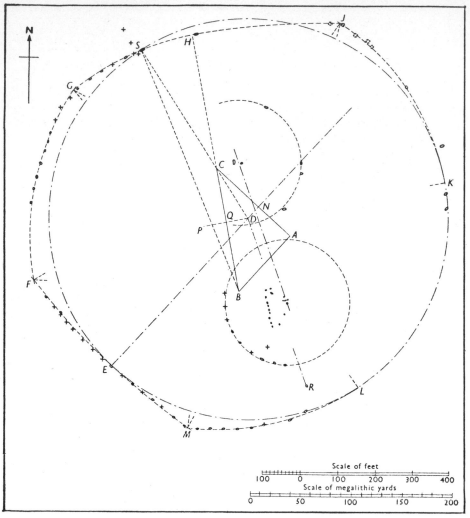

The geometry of Avebury (dots and dashes) on a survey of its stones (blobs: surviving stones; crosses: sockets for stones).

in places standing 8 metres above the present base of the ditch and 5 metres above the surrounding ground. It can be calculated that some 116,000 cubic metres of chalk must have been excavated from the ditch and piled up into the bank and that the work to do all this would have taken 200 men about 780 continuous days' work to complete. On to this total, as with Silbury Hill, must be added the large number of other people needed to feed, house and organize the work-force and to plan all aspects of the project from beginning to end.

Yet the excavation of the ditch and the building of the bank still amounted to only about half the total effort put into Avebury. Inside the ditched area are the sparse remnants of what was once the biggest stone circle known anywhere, about 355 metres in its maximum diameter. Although deliberate destruction in medieval and later times has sadly reduced this mighty ring, excavation has recovered the positions of many of

An avenue of standing stones runs from the 3rd millennium circles at Avebury up to the Sanctuary, the former site of wooden buildings of Avebury's date and of a subsequent double stone circle.

the stones and it seems likely that the main ring originally contained— assuming that it was completed—about 90 huge blocks of sarsen stone each weighing perhaps up to about 5 tonnes. There were two subsidiary circles inside the main one, each with a diameter of 103 metres. They might have contained 30 stones each to make the overall total perhaps 150. The effort needed to quarry, haul and roll these stones to the site from the Marlborough Downs several kilometres away, and then to set them up into their prepared sockets, must have been prodigious.

Moreover, the plan of the Avebury circles shows that their designers possessed a truly remarkable skill in field surveying and geometry. Professor Thom has shown that the three stone circles were set out on an exact geometrical plan which must have been surveyed and marked out on the site before the ditch was dug. The ditch follows the irregular shape of the outer circle very closely, confirming that the two features are part of a single plan, and it seems unlikely that the stones would have been hauled through the narrow entrances in the bank and then round to their chosen positions after the digging of the ditch.

To decide how close an inferred geometrical construction is likely to be to the one actually used by the designers of a site the geometry is drawn separately on a transparent sheet, to the same scale as the plan of the stones themselves, and then superimposed on the ground plan. In the case of Avebury the geometry, complicated though it seems at first sight, runs right through most of the remaining stones even though many of these were re-erected in their discovered sockets after Alexander Keiller's excavations of the 1930s.

The conclusion is that a classic Pythagorean right-angled triangle with sides in the proportion of 3, 4 and 5, measuring 75, 100 and 125 megalithic yards, was first laid out on the ground, the corners presumably being marked with stout pegs. Arcs of three large circles were then drawn, presumably with a stretched cord attached to the corner pegs, to form the north-east and south sides of the great circle. The arcs would have to have been checked frequently with measuring rods. Three of these radii were 260 megalithic yards long and the eastern side, though badly ruined, may have been composed of part of a circle 230 megalithic yards in diameter.

The arc of the south-western side (and possibly one on the north) is, however, part of a much larger circle with a radius of no less than 750 megalithic yards. The centre point for this is well off the site to the north-east and shows that the geometry of the Avebury rings was measured and surveyed out on to the ground before the bank and ditch were constructed. The bank runs right across this long radius. Very impressive too is the fact that all the arcs of the outer circle are very close to multiples of $2\frac{1}{2}$ megalithic yards in length; in many other smaller circles the perimeter has been found to be very close to whole numbers of these megalithic rods.

There are, unfortunately, no radiocarbon dates for Avebury, but from the fairly sparse archaeological evidence it seems likely to have been built in late Neolithic times, perhaps a few centuries after Stonehenge I and Silbury Hill.

Culmination at Stonehenge

Although it was into Avebury that our late Neolithic ancestors put their greatest amount of physical effort and geometrical ingenuity, it was at the much smaller site of Stonehenge that the architecture of the stone circles reached its peak. The second major stage of building there—in the late third millennium BC, judging from two radiocarbon dates—must be the most remarkable and spectacular achievement in prehistoric engineering and organization of which any evidence has come down to us. Eighty-two stones of grey-blue dolerite—quarried from a relatively small area in the Preseli mountains in south Wales—were roughly dressed and then transported about 300 kilometres to Wiltshire. There they were finally shaped and formed the first stone circle at Stonehenge, a double ring, probably of 38 pairs with 6 extra ones on the north-east forming a more complex entrance.

Numerous chips of the dolerite have been found all over the site in a thin layer on top of the primary silts in the henge ditch. These chips must have been produced by the final dressing and shaping of the stones and probably prior to their erection. In the same layer were occasional sherds of Beaker pottery showing that the first stone circle was built at this well defined point in the archaeological sequence of prehistoric Britain, perhaps at about 2400 or 2300 BC if dates for other Beaker sites are a guide.

The route by which these stones were probably brought has been worked out by Professor Richard Atkinson; most of the journey must have been by water—along rivers and the coast—it being much easier to transport heavy megaliths this way than overland. The popular idea that rafts were used to carry the bluestones has recently been questioned by Philip Banbury who has pointed out that such craft are slow, difficult to propel, unseaworthy and generally unsuitable for negotiating winds and tides. He suggests that it is much more likely that each block was carried on two or three dug-out canoes lashed together side by side.

At the site a broad processional road, flanked by ditches and known as the Avenue, was built, running up from the river Avon to approach Stonehenge from the north-east: the original entrance was widened to accommodate it. It is usually believed that the bluestones were hauled along this processional way on the final stage of their journey to Stonehenge, having been floated up the Avon from the south coast of England. The existence of the Avenue running down to the river by the shallowest route—exactly as one would expect if the bluestones were being brought this way from Wales—is a strong point (if one were needed) against the theory that ice sheets had deposited the stones on Salisbury Plain at a much earlier date. If it did the Avenue would be inexplicable.

The existence of the double circle of bluestones was not suspected until the excavations of the 1950s uncovered the sockets for it, known as the Q and R holes. The bluestones now stand in a different formation, the result of the final re-arrangement of the site some centuries later. Although most of the Q and R holes explored reveal pressure marks on their chalk bases, showing that heavy stones had stood in them for a period, yet the double

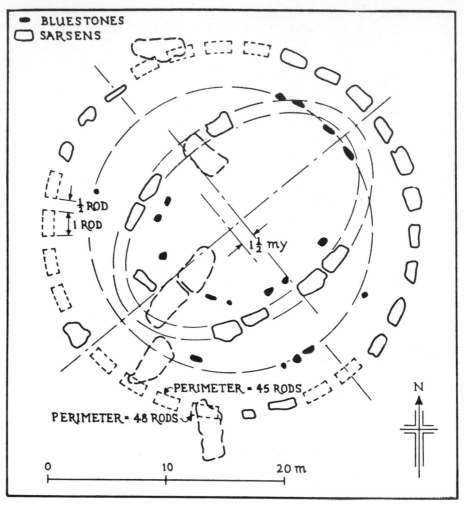

Plan and suggested geometry of the final building at Stonehenge.

circle was never finished. The last few holes remained undug and it seems that the plans for the site were suddenly changed before the monument was completed. It seems incredible that after the immense labour of bringing 82 megaliths from south Wales to Wiltshire, and after erecting most of them, the whole project should be abandoned in favour of a much more elaborate temple built of local sarsen stone, but this seems to be what happened. The bluestone rings must have been dismantled, and the megaliths taken off the site and stored somewhere nearby, before the 40 huge sarsen uprights (44 if the station stones are assumed to have been erected at this time) and their 35 massive lintels—having been brought about 24 kilometres from the Marlborough Downs to the north—were rolled ponderously on to the site and erected into the third Stonehenge.

This last major construction at the site produced a temple which is unique in prehistoric Europe and which has such a comparatively sophisticated architectural design that it is scarcely surprising that theories involving the bringing of skilled designers from the Mediterranean world have often been invoked in the past to explain it. Essentially the temple in its final form consists of an outer circle and an inner horseshoe. The outer circle originally had 30 upright stones capped with a continuous row of 30 lintels and the inner horseshoe consisted of five free-standing archways of three stones, known as trilithons. Many of the stones are carefully dressed to shape and all the lintels have two sockets which lock on to projecting knobs on top of the uprights. Each of the lintels of the outer circle has in addition a tongue at one end and a groove at the other with which it locks into its neighbours' ends. All of them are curved to match the curvature of the outer circle. Some of the huge uprights weigh 20 tonnes and are sunk 1·5 metres into the chalk.

Professor Thom discovered some hitherto unsuspected geometrical properties in the sarsen temple which reveal its design to be even more remarkable and elegant. The inside faces of the remaining stones of the outer ring—most of which have been carefully dressed to an even surface—fit remarkably well on to an accurately drawn true circle with a *perimeter* of exactly 45 megalithic rods ($112\frac{1}{2}$ megalithic yards). Each of the 30 uprights in this scheme is evenly spaced around the circle and occupies a space of 1 rod; each of the 30 gaps between them is half a rod, while the stones are all about half a rod thick. It is remarkable how closely the stones fit into these positions when the geometrical scheme is superimposed on the plan of the site. It is also interesting that the true north line exactly clips the ends of two of the opposing stone positions defined in this way. The 50° line, running through the middle of one of the archways, passes close to the Heel stone and to the centre of the Avenue (with a bearing of about 49° 36′).

The geometry of the horseshoe of trilithons is not quite so clear but the inside faces of the few uprights still in or close to their original positions fit very well round an ellipse with axes of 27 and 17 megalithic yards. The long axis of the ellipse, independently defined, also runs through the Heel stone archway of the outer circle just mentioned—that in which the midsummer sunrise is framed.

At the same time that the sarsen temple was built, or soon afterwards, the Welsh bluestones were built into a new monument, part of which consisted of at least one trilithon of dressed stone like those of the sarsen structure. The location of this second bluestone monument is unknown but it was eventually dismantled and the knobs on the uprights (to fit into the lintels) were battered off. Another double circle was then planned for the Welsh stones, this time possibly in the form of a geometrically constructed spiral just outside the sarsen outer circle. This ring was not finished either and its sockets—known as the Y and Z holes—were incomplete; they were also left open and abandoned to fill slowly with dust and silt. Presumably the bluestones were then built into the simple circle and horseshoe of standing stones, the sad remains of which are now visible at the site today.

The dating of these later phases of activity at Stonehenge is fairly clear, both from archaeological evidence and from radiocarbon measurements. Radiocarbon dates for the first and second stone temples, show that the double bluestone circle and the sarsen temple were built close together, probably towards the end of the third millennium BC. The final alteration of the site—involving the preparation and abandonment of the double spiral and, presumably, the building of the circle and horseshoe immediately afterwards—occurred much later, probably in the mid-second millennium BC.

From this dating there is an overwhelming probability that the great sarsen temple was built long before the Mycenaean period in Greece—conventionally thought to have begun in the mid-second millennium BC—so that it owes nothing to Mycenaean architects or influence, a theory much in favour in the 1950s and early 1960s. It must therefore be either a purely native creation or the result of the impact on Chalcolithic England of some as yet unidentified newcomers.

The limited amount of archaeological dating evidence fits this scheme. Sherds of Grooved ware—like that found at Durrington Walls and Skara Brae—came from the base of the ditch of Stonehenge I. In a slightly later layer of excavated material, the same as that in which occurred numerous chips of bluestone and which must mark the arrival of the first megaliths on the site, are found Beaker sherds. Radiocarbon dates from several other sites have shown that the earliest Beakers in Britain arrived soon after the middle of the third millennium BC. For the sarsen temple no direct archaeological evidence is available now that the Mycenaean connection has been broken but there is no reason to doubt the late third millennium date suggested by the radiocarbon evidence, nor the mid-second millennium date for the final alteration to the site.

The sarsen temple at Stonehenge is a truly remarkable building in every sense of the word. The careful shaping of the stones, the lintels fitted on to the uprights with mortice and tenon joints and the elegant simplicity of the geometrical construction underlying the stones all show that in Wiltshire the tradition of the stone-circle builders reached an abrupt and unique zenith. Stonehenge and Avebury together must surely represent the main centre of whatever society it was that evolved the geometry and astronomy of the stone circles and standing stones.

Durrington Walls

Within the last ten years three outstanding excavations in southern England, at Durrington Walls, Mount Pleasant and Marden, have revolutionized our knowledge of what else was going on in late Neolithic and Chalcolithic times apart from the construction of gigantic and sophisticated temple-observatories. Whereas all the henge monuments previously explored were much smaller and seem best interpreted as purely ritual sites with no signs, except at Woodhenge, of domestic occupation, these three large ones were different.

About 355 metres across, the outer circle at Avebury now ▶
encloses part of the medieval village.

Durrington Walls, situated about 4·8 kilometres north of Stonehenge, has yielded the most information. For the first time since excavation became a reasonably scientific procedure a henge monument was discovered which had both very large amounts of food and other domestic refuse associated with it and also evidence of massive roofed wooden buildings inside the enclosed area. As a result it has been argued that the missing segment in our picture of the late Neolithic society which evolved geometry, astronomy and religion to such a high level—the segment showing where people lived, trained and worked—has been filled in.

The site is now an inconspicuous earthwork half of which has been ploughed flat on the surface and is only visible in air photographs. It consists of an enclosure of about 10·1 hectares surrounded by a huge flat-bottomed ditch 5·64 metres deep in places and up to 12·8 metres wide at the top. The chalk excavated from this ditch was piled up into a bank outside it; this is now much denuded but is still 30 metres wide and must have been perhaps 2 metres or more high originally. The total length of the perimeter ditch is about 170 metres and the volume of chalk piled up has been estimated at about 50,000 cubic metres. Such a task would have occupied a gang of 200 men, armed with Neolithic equipment, full time for 440 days, a formidable project even by the standards of Silbury Hill and Avebury.

There are two entrances into the huge enclosure, on the north-west and south-east, and each consists of a causeway of undug chalk across the ditch and a corresponding gap in the bank in front of it. Excavations showed that the great ditch had completely filled up over the centuries with stratified deposits of weathered chalk and silt which had buried, and thus protected, masses of debris thrown in long ago when the henge was newly built.

Many antler picks were found lying on the flat floor of the ditch—where they had evidently been thrown immediately after the completion of the digging—and three of these gave radiocarbon dates which clustered closely in the mid-third millennium BC: this must be when the henge was built. At the terminal of the ditch, next to the entrance, was found a mass of refuse which must have begun to be tipped into the ditch very soon after it was dug. The deposits included large quantities of ash, broken animal bones, pieces of pottery and flints—all the usual debris of a domestic site. This discovery was a great surprise to the excavator at the time, as also to other interested archaeologists, as deposits of domestic refuse seemed difficult to reconcile with the ritual and ceremonial character assumed to belong to a henge monument.

About 27 metres in from one entrance were found a series of concentric rings of huge post-holes cut deeply into the chalk and a second set appeared 119 metres to the north. The former, the 'southern circle', was most informative. In most cases where the post-holes of wooden structures are preserved on the chalk downs the original floor, never buried very deeply below the turf, has been destroyed by later ploughing, leaving only the bases of the holes. Here, however, the site was at the bottom of a shallow valley and earth and silt had washed down over the centuries and covered the floor

◀ *About 90 sarsen stones each weighing some 5 tonnes originally made up the outer circle at Avebury.*

125

of the wooden building with an extra thickness of soil which had protected it. Thus everything was preserved just as it had been abandoned, perhaps 3,900 or 4,000 years ago.

From the way the rings of post-holes were laid out, and from a few examples of overlapping post-holes, it was possible to deduce that there had been two successive sets of posts on the site of the southern circle, presumably the remains of two distinct buildings. The first and oldest was 23 metres in diameter with four rings of posts while the second was larger and more elaborate—36 metres across with six concentric rings of uprights. The excavation of the post-holes themselves revealed that in both structures the timber uprights had rotted in position, leaving 'casts' of their shapes as cylinders of finer, looser soil among the packing of rammed chalk. Some of the oak timbers which once had stood there were very large, usually 30 to 38 centimetres in diameter and therefore perhaps weighing from 2 to 3 tonnes when fresh and green. The two massive door-posts were around 0·9 metres in diameter and must originally have weighed between 4 and 5 tonnes.

The posts of the earlier structure were packed with dirty, rammed chalk while those of the later one had a packing of lumps of fresh, clean chalk which must have come from the ditch. The radiocarbon ages of three of the antler picks found in some of the post-holes were exactly the same as those from the base of the ditch—in the mid-third millennium BC. This confirms that the henge and the second timber buildings were built at the same time so that the first one must have stood on the downs before the enclosing earthwork was made; it probably belongs to middle Neolithic times.

On the floor of the second building, mainly around the vanished posts and their sockets, were more large quantities of occupation debris similar to that found in the terminal of the ditch—potsherds, bones and flints. Outside what seemed to be the entrance (flanked by extra large posts) was a chalk rubble platform with many signs that it had perhaps been a cooking place or a dump for hot stones used in cooking—and there was a fireplace in the centre of the building.

The first question for the excavator to decide was whether the southern wooden building had been roofed or whether it was some kind of open temple, perhaps like a timber version of Stonehenge. The quantities of refuse contrasted with the few artefacts found in most other henge sites and themselves suggested that these were roofed buildings; however, ceremonies involving meals and depositions of flints could conceivably have taken place in an open temple. A careful analysis of the timber traces of the second construction by C. M. Musson, an architect, showed that the size and spacing of both sets of rings and of the individual timbers in them was quite consistent with the plans of two large roundhouses having pitched roofs of timber, presumably covered with thatch. This was even clearer in the northern roundhouse where the sizes of the posts were much greater than would have been strictly necessary to support a roof of the diameter needed. Here the four massive central posts could have supported a raised lantern in the centre to let light in, and smoke out.

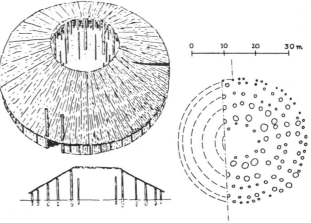

Within a non-defensive ditch at Dur-rington Walls, not far from Stonehenge in southern England, are the post-holes (above) of circular wooden buildings (right) and signs of thorough-going domestic occupation of the mid-3rd millennium BC. For the first time an enclosure of the kind usually encompassing an apparently only ritual area showed how the people of the time, perhaps the circle builders themselves, actually lived.

127

This giant henge site thus contained at least two really large wooden roofed buildings (with others perhaps awaiting discovery) but there was no archaeological precedent at the time of its excavation for finding what appeared to be a unique combination of the features of a supposedly ritual or ceremonial henge site and those of a domestic site; the two groups of features seemed to contradict one another.

A variety of analogies could be drawn from modern experience and observation of primitive peoples to assist in the interpretation of Durrington Walls. Dr Wainwright, for example, at first favoured a comparison with the large, eighteenth-century round council houses of the Creek Indians of Georgia, which were observed in use by European travellers, and one of which—the Irene Mound site, Georgia—was excavated in the 1930s. These were public and ceremonial buildings, built on concentric circles of posts and surprisingly similar in design to the Durrington Walls roundhouses; they were used only on special occasions when ceremonies involving much drinking took place followed by the deliberate smashing of the drinking vessels and their deposition in a midden outside.

But might the site have been a military kraal for young warriors, similar to those housing Cetewayo's dreaded *impi* which were burned by British troops in the Zulu war of 1879? Or could it be the carefully demarcated Neolithic equivalent of a monastery and training college, a place of residence where professional priests or wise men lived, worked and trained? Or could it be a colonial settlement of foreigners recently arrived in Britain?

There is no doubt that the concept of a ceremonial centre for astronomers, priests and wise men—rather like those built by the Maya people in central America during the first millennium BC—would fit the evidence very neatly. It explains everything about the site as well as making much more plausible all of Professor Thom's discoveries. With this theory there is no need to doubt or ignore large segments of the available evidence. Such a special community of religious and wise men might well be set apart from the rest of the peasant population by a massive earthwork, much as the Early Christian monasteries often were 3,000 years later: the 'ritual' features of the henge are thus well explained. The ashes, bones, flints and potsherds, together with the signs of cooking, would be similarly accounted for if a permanent community inhabited the site: this would explain the 'domestic' features found. Lastly and most important, the discovery of large, inhabited ceremonial centres like Durrington Walls fills in the second half of the picture outlined by the work of Professor Thom. It was always difficult to accept such advanced intellectual skills as were claimed to be reflected by the standing stones when there was no sign among the rest of the many sites of the same period of the kind of society which could have organized the work on a nationwide basis.

Chapter IX   Methods
of Interpretation

The archaeological evidence for the more spectacular of the megalith builders' activities in various parts of the western Mediterranean and Atlantic Europe has raised more than one fundamental problem of prehistoric studies. For example, the earliest of them is now dated to the fifth millennium BC, 2,000 years or more earlier than was thought only a quarter of a century ago. At that time it seemed very likely that the builders of the megalithic chambered mounds were the contemporaries of the city-dwelling, Early Bronze Age civilizations of the eastern Mediterranean and it was possible to imagine them as impoverished colonists from that urban world who had reverted to a Stone Age technology because of the great distance from the homeland and poor communications. Now, however, thanks to new dating based on calibrated radiocarbon measurements, some entirely new explanation of the first great phase of megalith building is needed.

The very concept of 'explanations' of prehistoric archaeological material poses another basic problem, however: how are such explanations devised? How do we know what sort of people put up massive buildings and made tools and weapons during the long, silent millennia before written records provide contemporary descriptions of vanished peoples? Indeed can we really *know* anything about these things, or simply make informed guesses?

The scientific method

In a scientific discipline like biology or physics the processes by which knowledge and understanding are advanced are well known. There are several clear stages in research, leading from the first observations of new facts right up to the eventual formulation of new theories and even laws. The first two stages are the *collection* of all kinds of evidence and its *classification*. The process of classification should reveal patterns and regularities in the collected facts (if there are enough of them) and should lead on to the third stage, the framing of *hypotheses* (explanations). It is at this point, according to many scientists, that the scientific process most resembles an art, relying on intuition and inspiration; ideas and explanations can flash into minds saturated with information and long familiarity with all its details. True science is, however, distinguished from false by the following fourth and fifth stages in which the *implications* of the new hypotheses (not yet elevated to the status of formal theories) are *defined* and *tested* respectively. The entire success of science, and the activity which distinguishes the scientific worker from all others, no matter what is the subject being studied, depends on this capacity to define the predictions made by an hypothesis and then to think of experiments and tests to discover whether these predictions are correct or not. The hypothesis whose predictions are repeatedly verified survives. It may ultimately be elevated to the status of a formal theory and may perhaps give rise in the long run to a scientific law. The hypothesis whose predictions are not borne out has either to be discarded or modified: in the latter case new predictions are made and tested in the same way.

A 'natural science' dealing with present-day phenomena usually has no difficulty in pursuing stages 4 and 5, assuming that it has a good supply of competent workers and reasonable funds. If more material or information is needed to work on, this can be bought or collected. If the solutions to its problems are not clear-cut, statistical techniques can be invoked to sort out reliable from unreliable deductions. In other words, the process by which the hypotheses, the theories and ultimately the laws of such sciences are formed is a continuous circular one. It starts with the collection of information and its classification, it then goes on to devising preliminary explanations, defines the predictions and implications of these hypotheses and finally proceeds to go back to the evidence to test the predictions, modifying the hypotheses in the light of the results of the tests and so on. The scientist concerned is always able to proceed directly from observations to hypothesis and back again. However, this is unfortunately not the case with the interpretation in social terms of the facts of prehistoric archaeology and it is very important to understand this basic difference between the historical and the other sciences.

The archaeological method

Prehistoric archaeology is a set of techniques for finding, recovering, preserving and analysing those fragments of the material creations of vanished, pre-literate human societies which time and circumstance have allowed to survive (these fragments may be said to include not only things made or altered by man but also traces of the effects his activities had on the natural environment). By itself archaeology can tell us nothing directly about society. The part of the material culture of a vanished society— everything it made, or left physical traces of—which has actually survived the millennia to become the archaeological record is usually a very small one. We cannot assume that the most important part, or even a representative part, has been preserved to be discovered by modern archaeologists.

More important still is the fact that the organism which created the culture has now vanished completely and beyond recall. This organism was a population of living people bound together by common genetic, linguistic and cultural ties and by a complex and evolving web of social relationships. Most human artefacts—tools and weapons, clothes, containers, ornaments and buildings—were the products of this working social organism and can only be fully understood as part of that once-living entity. Without it they become random and disarticulated fragments, quite devoid of social meaning *in themselves*. They might be thought of as analogous to the few scattered and rusting fragments of a motor car on a Hebridean beach. To an observer in AD 3000, ignorant of the internal combustion engine, these pieces of iron might reveal nothing of the finely tuned mechanism which once spun along the highways of the 1970s, *unless* he either had contemporary descriptions of the workings of a car or knew enough of twentieth-century engineering from other sources to make an intelligent guess about the purpose of the fragments.

The situation with prehistoric archaeological evidence is similar in principle but even more difficult for the investigator to untangle. The complex social organization which created the fragments concerned has vanished beyond recall just as the abandoned motor car has long been dismantled and most of its fragments scattered and robbed. However, while the basic design of all vehicles using the internal combustion engine is much the same—so that a good guess could be made at the original form of our Hebridean wreck (given a minimum knowledge of engineering)—the situation with human societies is quite different.

During the 4 million years or so that man has been on the Earth he has devised such a huge variety of social organizations, customs and institutions that, while some broad general patterns are apparent, no really reliable automatic and detailed correlations are possible between material cultures and social organizations even in modern and historically known societies. In the case of prehistoric societies the difficulties of making such correlations are obviously far greater since no general laws linking the two sides of human culture are yet known. Thus it is impossible to proceed directly from the archaeological evidence to the detailed reconstruction of the vanished societies which produced it.

How then are social explanations devised by archaeologists of prehistoric societies (that is, people about whom no written records are available)? The answer is, by *analogy*—by looking at the known primitive peoples who possess a material culture similar to the prehistoric one. This is obviously quite a different method of framing hypotheses and explanations from that employed by biologists and physicists who work directly from the facts to the explanations and then back to the facts again in order to test the explanations. The archaeologist collects the facts but gets his social explanations *indirectly* by drawing analogies with recent societies; there is no way that these hypotheses can be directly tested against the prehistoric archaeological evidence.

If we find a bronze object looking like a spearhead in a prehistoric burial ground we assume it is one because it looks like a modern spear. Yet we cannot know for certain that its Bronze Age owner thought of it or used it as a spear because we cannot ask him. The strict limits imposed on archaeological interpretation by the function of analogy are plain when one is faced with more complex archaeological phenomena such as a prehistoric site or structure with artefacts scattered around and in it. Many of the monuments known as megalithic or chambered tombs have been found to contain human bones—often in positions which show that the older skeletons had been re-arranged—as well as a variety of artefacts such as potsherds, flint implements and so on. Remains of fires are sometimes found in the front of the entrance to the megalithic chamber as well as within it and this doorway—in Britain at least—was usually blocked up when the 'tomb' had ceased to be used. The presence of human remains has naturally given rise to the belief that these megalithic monuments were tombs and that the artefacts in them were grave goods meant to accompany the dead to the next world. Further assumptions have followed—for example that the dark interior of the chamber represented to the builders the womb of the Earth Mother goddess to which her children return at death, and also that the tombs were communal ones used by the whole community.

However, it must be clear that the only undoubted *facts* available are the nature of the cairn and its megalithic chamber—its size, ground plan, design, dimensions and so on—and the various layers, objects and human remains associated with it. In the absence of written records we clearly cannot know that the builders of this megalithic construction even thought of it primarily as a tomb: it might have been to them a place of sacrifice, or a war memorial or a prehistoric equivalent of a medieval abbey or cathedral, the main purpose of which was to serve as a temple but in which the great ones of the day were entitled to be buried. It is quite plain that the interpretations we put on the megaliths have to be derived by analogy—from what the archaeologist thinks is a likely function for them in the light of his knowledge of the whole later history of buildings and structures. No matter how long a specific view has been held about a class of archaeological sites, nor how eminent or well versed in novel techniques are those holding that view, it may still be completely erroneous, and ripe for replacement by another interpretation which explains more of the facts better.

There is thus a strict limit on what can be *directly* inferred from prehistoric archaeological evidence and it is important to remember this when considering a broad topic such as the origin and nature of the megalith builders and their creations. Radiocarbon dates show how old many of the megaliths are—and thus suggest the probable order in which they appeared—and experiment can prove how much effort was expended in setting up the massive stones. The various structural types can be identified and their geographical distribution plotted and compared with other archaeological objects of the same age. The contents of the 'tombs' can be identified and studied and the way they were arranged in the sepulchres analysed, sometimes to reveal a sequence of burials. But the social purpose and context of the whole vast Mediterranean and Atlantic European megalithic phenomenon—involving the construction of thousands of massive stone buildings and, later, the setting up of thousands of standing stones—has to be inferred in quite a different way.

The megaliths clearly represent a very significant development in prehistoric Europe—marking a tremendous physical and, later, intellectual achievement. Yet to understand them in social terms we have to look beyond the archaeological evidence to studies of modern societies and modern human behaviour as well as to historical records. The question then arises, what are the preferable analogies to be drawn with the megaliths and—more fundamentally—what is known about the principles of the evolution of early societies that might help to explain them? But it is an awkward fact that there seem to be two quite different views about how man and society have developed and changed, a division which is hardly discussed at all in the context of prehistoric archaeology but which affects all social interpretations, to a greater or lesser extent, of modern society as well as of ancient.

The evolution of societies

How man developed his modern societies was first tackled systematically in modern times by Jean-Jacques Rousseau who in 1753 opened his *Discourse on the origin of inequality among men* with the words: 'I conceive that there are two kinds of inequality among the human species; one, which I call natural or physical, because it is established by nature . . . and another, which may be called moral or political inequality because it depends on a kind of convention, and is established, or at least authorized by the consent of men.' He concluded that most inequality had arisen in man since his departure from the 'state of nature' where there is little. However he made an important distinction between inequality *between* peoples or races—which he considered ineradicable and fixed by nature—and that between individuals and classes of the *same* society which he thought artificial. These latter differences were assumed to have arisen as societies developed, as a result of the different needs of a variety of pursuits and activities in a complex organization.

This is a social version of the biological theory of evolution subsequently developed by Lamarck which held that different physical characteristics appear and disappear as a result of their use and disuse in specific environments. The social version of this theory was widely accepted, as it still is today, and seems to have influenced even the founder of modern evolutionary theory, Charles Darwin. When Darwin formulated the law of natural selection in *The Origin of Species* in 1859, to give the principle of evolution its first scientific foundation, he avoided the question of the development of human societies both in this work and later in *The Descent of Man*, presumably because it was too controversial.

Karl Marx presented the Lamarckian view of social evolution in classical form. In the *Communist Manifesto*, which he wrote with Friedrich Engels in 1848, he outlined the past development of society in terms of the rise in each period of the most advanced class, which would achieve dominance and introduce reforms and innovations only to stagnate and become reactionary, eventually to be replaced by a new set of innovators. Thus the feudal order was gradually replaced by the rule of the middle classes (the bourgeoisie) which had grown up on trade and commerce and whose innovative abilities then produced the Industrial Revolution. According to the laws of evolution the bourgeoisie was to be replaced in its turn, since it had become reactionary, by the very working class which its activities had called into being. The rise to power of the working class (or proletariat)—at first by way of increased misery and oppression—would ultimately end injustice and oppression and bring about an egalitarian and class-less society.

For present purposes the most crucial of Marx's theories is that which forecasts the *future* state of society, after the final revolution in its long history had overthrown the bourgeoisie and brought the progressive working classes to power. Although Marx was not too specific about the details of these future developments he did make some comments, mainly in the *Critique of the Gotha programme*. He held that, after this revolution and assumption of power by the proletariat, there would be a transitional stage in which the apparatus of the capitalist state would be broken up and re-modelled to permit a rational planning of the economy (the 'dictatorship of the proletariat'). Eventually, however, a higher order of society would develop in which the evils of capitalism would disappear: the majority of the population—transformed in outlook and attitudes towards life and work—would be regarded as members of the proletariat and even the apparatus of the state itself would gradually wither away because it was no longer needed. Marx was here putting forward the classic Lamarckian doctrine as applied to human society—that when the environment changed the nature of man himself would change. Crime, prostitution, oppression and exploitation would all disappear since the state of capitalism which had produced these evils would itself have disappeared. Thus the division of society into classes was an unnatural condition, the product of an oppressive system; it too should vanish with the disappearance of the capitalist state.

Most modern socialist and liberal political thought—as well as much of the thinking underlying the supposedly scientific investigation of Man himself—makes this fundamental assumption, that the evils and inequalities in a given modern society are the result of the unjust nature of that society and could be made to disappear if the social environment was suitably changed. The entire moral basis of egalitarianism must rest on this belief, that it is unjust for one group of people to be better off than another, or to be ruling it, because this upper class is exploiting people who could be rulers themselves given the right opportunity. Much modern psychology, behavioural science, educational theory and many other social scientific disciplines rely heavily on the Lamarckian view of social development. Perhaps the most extreme academic form of this doctrine was the concept of the *tabula rasa* which appeared in psychological studies in the early years of

Archaeological excavation may reveal the surface of a settlement site (above) or cut a clear section through it (below) and find human remains and human belongings, but there is a limit to what can be directly inferred from that evidence about a prehistoric people.

this century. According to this idea the mind of every newborn child was a 'blank slate' on which habits, ideas and emotions were gradually inscribed by its environment from the moment of birth: hereditary influences were ruled out and the corollary of the theory was that every individual has an equal potential. At present even the concept of innate differences between the races of mankind themselves—as well as between individuals and classes within societies—is under attack from some quarters as an injustice and an offence against morality.

Archaeological theory is rarely explicit about the sources from which it derives the social interpretations of its data except when its practitioners are citizens of communist countries, but a little investigation shows the Lamarckian view to be paramount. V. G. Childe was explicit and set out his assumptions clearly in the final chapter of *Social evolution* (1951). In contrasting organic with cultural evolution he says: 'Cultural changes take place much more expeditiously (than organic). An individual member of a society discovers or invents a new device—or it may be a new pattern, a new song or a new rite. The discoverer or inventor can immediately impart it by precept and example to other members of his society. If he can convince them of its utility or virtue—if that is, society approves the innovation—it will then be adopted generally by the society, whose culture will be enriched and changed to that extent. . . . For the cultural innovation could be adopted by a whole population in less than one generation.' And later: 'But the process need not stop there. Inventions can be transmitted from one society to another, and that is precisely what diffusion means. But that is just what is impossible in organic evolution.' Childe's idea of diffusion as primarily a process of copying by one group of a new ideas or technique possessed by another, rather than by the actual dispersal of individuals possessing the new knowledge, is shown by a later comment: 'Diffusion generally means the adoption by one independent society of innovations initiated by another'. This clearly shows that the idea that a human culture exists independently of human physical attributes is firmly held.

The Lamarckian view is even clearer in the approach to the interpretation of European and British prehistory of many of the younger British archaeologists. It is fundamental, for example to the views of Colin Renfrew who, in *Before Civilisation* (1973), sought to show that a new interpretation of cultural development in prehistoric Europe had been made necessary by the correction backwards of radiocarbon dates by the tree-ring chronology. Because the radiocarbon dates for the earliest megaliths, for example, have to be made older by about 8 centuries it appears that these structures were being put up well before 4000 BC. They have thus become far older than the Early Bronze Age tombs of the eastern Mediterranean which were once thought to be their ancestors, and older even than the historical dates for the earliest cities in the Mesopotamian delta. The Atlantic European megaliths should thus be looked on as an entirely European phenomenon owing nothing to the rise of civilized city life in the Near East and the eastern Mediterranean. The same conclusions, according to

Renfrew, can be drawn from the appearance of the first European metallurgical industry in the Balkans; the radiocarbon dates, when given the necessary backward correction by about four centuries, show that the first Balkan coppersmiths were casting tools and weapons before 4000 BC, and that this could have been the result of a series of discoveries in south-east Europe and independent of the rise of metallurgy in Anatolia at about the same time.

The implications of these and other alterations in the chronology of important prehistoric European developments are clear to Renfrew; the old diffusionist explanations for the prehistory of the continent, as most recently defined by Childe, no longer hold good. The diffusionists believed that most technological advances took place first in the early cities of Mesopotamia (though metallurgy was probably pioneered in the ore-rich Anatolian highlands) and were then gradually spread outwards by example from these centres into the more backward lands around. In place of this 'modified diffusionism' of Childe (contrasting with earlier diffusionism which believed actual migrations on a large scale had taken place), Renfrew offers the concept of independent development, saying categorically: 'the movements and migration of peoples are no longer acceptable as explanations for the changes seen in the archaeological record.' The various examples given— which include the phenomenon of the megaliths, the first metallurgy in the Balkans and the designing and building of Stonehenge—are interpreted in terms of the local evolution of separate communities, exploiting and responding to their environments in a variety of ways. Indeed the concept of archaeology apparently held by many of the so-called 'new archaeologists' leads inevitably to this approach since it seems to involve the study of each culture and site mainly in terms of the relations and responses of the ancient peoples to their social and physical environment, of their exploitation of natural resources, their trading relations with neighbours and so on. Each prehistoric community seems to be visualized as geographically static but evolving in its own right in a variety of ways.

The underlying assumptions of this view are never explicitly stated by Renfrew, perhaps because they are considered to be beyond argument. Yet the theory is obviously the Lamarckian approach to social evolution in its most extreme form. No reason is apparently seen for doubting that any society anywhere—given the right conditions—could have developed from its own technological resources a series of innovations of almost any kind. The unfolding of the prehistory of the European continent in this way could be visualized as a dark landscape being lit by a succession of geographically random flashes—each representing the sparks of isolated genius. By contrast the older view imagined the dark continent as being steadily more irradiated by the gradually spreading light from the civilized orient. The non-diffusionist view is of course helped by the fact that the traces of foreigners and immigrants which have been detected in the archaeological record in the past are usually ambiguous and incomplete and by the clear possibility that any such immigrants who did arrive could well have modified their skills and traditions drastically in response to their new environment. Nevertheless, this view of cultural development really goes back to the old pre-Darwin special creation theory as applied to human societies: instead of the spontaneous appearance of animal species created by God we now have the spontaneous appearance of new ideas and skills created by Man. Both views equally decisively reject the influences of hereditary factors and this extreme anti-diffusionist view might be said to be the archaeological version of the *tabula rasa* theory of psychology— visualizing each prehistoric community as waiting to flower with genius if its environment was favourable.

The question now arises—are these very large assumptions justified? Are separate societies (prehistoric and modern), and separate groups and classes within societies, solely the product of environment and circumstance or are they themselves the end products of the adaptation to varying environments of groups of people with varying inherited qualities? Could the normal laws of evolution and natural selection still be acting on individuals and on societies in the same way as they have done on the races of man and on the animal species themselves? In other words did these evolutionary laws really become suspended for Man once he had reached a certain level of cultural development and did his enormous brain and his self-diagnosed Free Will then purposefully take over and supplant natural selection?

The alternative interpretation of the evolution of man and society is that these laws have not been suspended at all—that social development should not be regarded as entirely a thing apart from and above the effects of physical evolution but, in part at least, as an extension of it. T. H. Huxley had one of the finest scientific minds of the nineteenth century and he took up this very problem. Discussing Rousseau's idea that there were two kinds of inequality, he wrote: 'Before drawing this sharp line of demarcation between natural and political inequality, might it not be as well to enquire whether they are not intimately connected, in such a manner that the latter is essentially a consequence of the former?' He then discussed the numerous differences which were observable in children from the earliest age, even among those of one (large Victorian) family, and how these affected social relationships.

But this was near the end of the nineteenth century and before the science of genetics had become properly established, and since Huxley's time the mechanisms of genetic mutation and recombination have been defined, exactly described and applied to the elucidation of many biological and physiological problems. Genetics provided the mechanism for Darwin's 'random variation' of physical characteristics which he had assumed— without evidence at the time—must exist for natural selection to work on. Thus the second major school in the study of human social development is an evolutionary one, founded by another great nineteenth-century thinker, Herbert Spencer (he was also criticized, by historians, for ignoring man's Free Will). It is Darwinian as opposed to Lamarckian (more Darwinian in fact than Darwin himself!) since it now holds that, in addition to environmental factors, evolutionary mechanisms work on inherited characteristics to separate out individuals and classes within societies as well as to separate races and species over much longer time spans.

The Darwinian approach has been applied to general accounts of man's development, for example by H. G. Wells and Carleton S. Coon. However the meaning of this approach for the detailed interpretation of archaeological problems has hardly been touched on, not least perhaps because genetically orientated studies are now widely unpopular in some quarters when they are applied to man and his supposed Free Will. This dogmatic Lamarckian attitude to heritability in Man was well described by Coon when he was discussing race: 'More serious are the activities of the academic de-bunkers and soft-pedallers who operate inside anthropology itself. Basing their ideas on the concept of the brotherhood of man, certain writers, who are mostly social anthropologists, consider it immoral to study race and produce book after book exposing it as a 'myth'. Their argument is that because the study of race once gave ammunition to racial fascists, who misused it, we should pretend that races do not exist.'

A similar kind of alarm is aroused nowadays by the idea that classes within societies may be in part genetically based, even though this by no means implies that they are fixed and immutable, only that natural and social selection are still playing their parts in human evolution.

Implications for prehistory
The most recent and detailed attempt to explain human prehistory and history by combining the evidence of archaeology, anthropology, history and genetics was made by C. D. Darlington in *The Evolution of Man and Society*. Evolution by natural and artificial selection continues to operate in all societies to bring about the separation of groups and classes as these try to gravitate towards the occupations and habitats that best suit them. Although the fundamental changes in inherited qualities are by the *mutation* of the genes themselves this is a rare, random and unpredictable process. Much more important for mankind, he suggests, is the *recombination* of the immensely varied human gene pool by breeding between previously isolated groups and the consequent appearance of hybrids. Numerous recorded examples appear to show quite clearly that periods of innovation and rapid development in the past have coincided with hybridization between hitherto separate populations or classes. In other words the recombination of talents and skills which then occurs produces a variety of new men with novel talents, some of whom respond to new situations successfully. The corollary of this—again documented with numerous examples—is that groups and classes within societies have a clear genetic basis and tend to be rigid or fluid according to how much or how little breeding between them occurs, and to how much opportunity is allowed for the movement of individuals between classes. After a period of hybridization between hitherto separate groups stability tends to set in with the new varieties of men coalescing into separate

layers or classes and perpetuating themselves as such by adopting more or less strict rules of inbreeding which make sure that marriage outside the class is not common. Time and again in man's history, Darlington believes, great changes and advances have come about through hybridization and out-breeding and stagnation has then occurred through later in-breeding.

A clear distinction—and one crucial to the problem of the megalith builders—has to be made between the evolution of peoples in this sense during the earliest, most primitive era of man's prehistory and that during the time of the more advanced early urban societies. A Palaeolithic hunting group—or a community of Neolithic farmers in newly colonized, nearly empty land—is likely to have become thoroughly adapted to its environment and way of life by natural selection for a variety of reasons, all connected with ability, in order to survive. Those abilities which make for success in hunting or farming are few and easily defined and will be selected for in the normal evolutionary way (a bad hunter or a bad farmer in a primitive society is more likely to starve and leave no progeny). Centuries or millennia of such selection—with extinction as the penalty for less good adaption in such isolated environments—as well as restricted possibilities for out-breeding (with its consequent inflow of new genes) are likely to result in such societies becoming highly specialized and homogeneous both culturally and genetically. During the whole of the Palaeolithic and Mesolithic periods—and in the early stages of Neolithic times in each new area affected by the agricultural revolution—the process must have been one of the constant separation and diversification of individual human groups— ultimately to the level of racial distinction—all closely adapted to their various environments and modes of life. Major exceptions to this process would doubtless occur at times of forced migrations, as when drastic changes in climate, like the onset and ending of glacial periods, occurred and also, on a smaller scale, when the new Neolithic farmers met and mingled with bands of Mesolithic hunters.

When one views human physical and cultural development in this way—in terms of adaptation and natural selection—some archaeological problems can be seen in a new light. For example, could the remarkable homogeneity of the early Neolithic Danubian culture over wide areas of central Europe in the sixth and fifth millennia BC have been the result of the genetic homogeneity of the first Danubian farmers themselves and of the fact that, before their hybridization with bands of Mesolithic forest dwellers, they may all have been descended from the one or two families (themselves hybrids no doubt) which successfully transferred and adapted the farming economy of the Mediterranean zone of south-east Europe into the temperate zone further north? Since these people were the first farmers in this zone it is reasonable to suppose that they quickly multiplied to fill their new, almost empty ecological niche. Hence we find that Danubian sites and equipment are almost identical from the regions of the middle Danube itself right across to the Netherlands, a distance of some 800 kilometres. Neither the pottery ('bandkeramik') nor the stone tools, nor the great wooden

Professor A. S. Thom at one end of the Grand Menhir Brisé, a ▶ toppled megalith in Brittany.

longhouses can be exactly matched among the Neolithic cultures further south-east in the Balkans, in the zone of the older Neolithic cultures from which the Danubians must have sprung and derived their domesticated cereals and animals.

Quite a different situation is apparent, however, in advanced societies. The crucial point—as described by V. G. Childe in *Man makes himself*—must have come when a Neolithic population of farmers and herdsmen was persuaded or coerced into producing more food than it needed so that a proportion of the people could specialize full time in non-farming activities—by being priests, wise men, merchants, chiefs, warriors and so on. From this point onwards an entirely new set of opportunities would have existed for individuals with unusual talents to flourish in: whereas previously these people might only have been indifferent farmers they might now be successful traders or persuasive priests. The development of the first true urban societies in Mesopotamia (and probably in the Nile delta in Egypt a little later) must have been both the result of and have accelerated this process as more and more surplus wealth and food was accumulated, first apparently in the temples and later in the granaries and treasuries of city rulers and kings with wider authority, and as an ever larger proportion of the population became specialized in non-agricultural pursuits.

This second great stage in Man's early evolution thus contrasts sharply with the first diversifying stage in the relatively sudden appearance of a wide range of new opportunities, and of the new men to take them. This process was doubtless accelerated in each new region where towns were established by migrating traders and other itinerant specialists. Instead of the constant separation of populations into distinctive racial and linguistic groups in the primary stage, we now have the recombination on a massive scale of individuals and groups of many origins into the early urban populations to form professional classes in stratified and genetically heterogeneous societies.

The results of this recombination and emergence of specialized groups is seen in the archaeological record. Evidence appears of monumental buildings, sculpture, fine pottery, widespread trading, writing, mathematics, astronomical and calendrical studies, sophisticated religions with elaborate temples, war machines and professional armies and so on. Although the new classes must originally have come into being by the extensive recombination of varied individuals and groups (originally from the country) and by the selection of the resulting hybrids for their various talents, there is abundant documentation that such classes subsequently perpetuate themselves in a stratified society by inbreeding and genetic isolation.

The implications for prehistoric Europe of this view of the close relationship between human physical and social evolution are plain. Once urban civilization had arisen and got under way in the Near East—and, later, in Palestine, Crete and the Aegean—the rise of advanced complex stratified societies, having many different specialists, must have progressed rapidly. Darlington's view is that the spread of civilization outwards from its

Rows of standing stones at Carnac in Brittany diminish in size in a definite direction.

Monumental buildings are often evidence that a society has begun to support specialists of one sort or another, as was the case in Early Dynastic Mesopotamia (above and below).

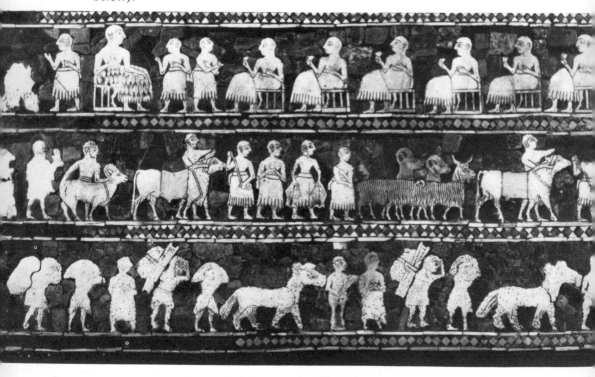

primary centres was the result of the actual movement of members of these skilled city-born classes as the old towns of the deltas gradually decayed (the farming populations, as always, stayed put). If this was so, the question is: did this spread of skilled new urban men continue beyond the zone of the Early Bronze Age towns of the Mediterranean into Neolithic Europe? The Darwinian view of the close link between drastic cultural change and hybridization suggests that a phenomenon like the appearance of the megalith builders could be a classic case of arrival of skilled and influential specialists, even if only in small numbers. However, such a theory, if it had to assume an urban origin for such specialists, would have to explain the startlingly early dates which we now have for the first megaliths. These have now been put back to a time before any outward spread of urban specialists could have occurred!

Recalling the main features of the two great phases of European megalith building it must now be decided which of the two fundamentally different explanations of the great cultural changes involved—broadly described here as the Lamarckian or the Darwinian—fits the archaeological facts better.

Chapter X   The Meaning of the Megaliths

A map of the occurrence of tombs containing evidence of the collective or communal burial rite in Neolithic and Chalcolithic times shows a remarkably consistent and straightforward maritime distribution throughout the Mediterranean and Atlantic Europe, extending as far as the North Sea and the Baltic. This distribution of the graves, and their approximate contemporaneity, both strongly suggest that there was a basic cultural link, and perhaps a genetic one, between the people buried in them.

But the vast majority of the collective tombs on the European mainland and in the British Isles—from Iberia northwards—are artificial stone chambers inside built mounds whereas the smaller numbers further east in the Mediterranean area tend to be mostly rock-cut tombs. In that sense therefore the megalith builders were very clearly a western and northern European phenomenon and the question is whether they, and their rite of collective burial, arose somewhere in Europe or whether people and rite arrived there from further east, undergoing a profound cultural metamorphosis when on the mainland. Some further considerations of the Maltese Chalcolithic temple-building culture are a useful start.

Malta

What conclusions can reasonably be drawn from the manner in which the megalith-building culture on Malta developed? There can be little doubt that Chalcolithic Malta saw either the arrival or the emergence of a professional priesthood and the rise of a small but skilled class of megalith builders—of architects and engineers—and of stone-decorating craftsmen who served this élite. In other words, on a small scale in Malta occurred a similar process to that attested in several other proto-urban and primitive hierarchical societies whereby a theocratic upper class was able to concentrate enough influence, power and wealth in its own hands to support itself in comfort, to employ a few skilled professionals to build, decorate and maintain its sanctuaries and regularly to recruit mass labour from among the agricultural population to do the heavy work of temple-building. If, of the two fundamentally different theories of human social evolution, a version of the Lamarckian theory is correct, then there can be no objection to supposing that the temple-building culture somehow spontaneously developed on Malta for purely local reasons. J. D. Evans favoured this view and Colin Renfrew drew a more specific analogy with the chiefdom societies found by the first Europeans on reaching many Polynesian islands. On the other hand, the opposing Darwinian view would not normally expect a small, isolated community of Neolithic peasant farmers—the product of evolutionary selection over many generations for their attachment to their flocks and land and to the simple ideologies of weather and fertility—suddenly to evolve such a stratified society spontaneously or to embark on the construction of monumental buildings. Rather would it expect to see evidence for the arrival of a small group of dominant people of some kind, its establishment on the island and probably its transformation by intermarriage with the leading aboriginal families into an entirely new local ruling class. From that time onwards the steady development of a Chalcolithic Maltese stratified society, with an increasingly impressive local tradition of monumental building to illustrate the power and prestige of the ruling groups, would not be surprising. Is there any evidence that something like this last did happen on Malta or is the archaeological evidence better explained by some version of the Lamarckian theory of indigenous local development?

The entire weight of the Maltese archaeological evidence favours the view that the temple-building culture evolved entirely on the islands and was not imported; the evolution of small temples into large ones, and the development and perfection of the local brand of megalithic architecture, is too clear and plausible for any other view to be seriously entertained. Similarly the Chalcolithic pottery—like the Neolithic wares before it is characteristically Maltese; occasional similarities are to be seen with Sicilian wares but they are no more than can be explained by casual contacts. Likewise the megalithic architecture itself cannot be precisely, or even generally, matched anywhere else although there are some general and potentially important similarities with the megalithic tombs of western Europe. But did the initial stimulus which set this evolution going come from outside in the form of ship-borne foreigners? One very striking fact has emerged only after the most recent research and is very difficult to reconcile with the concept of a totally indigenous cultural development. Throughout the whole of the long Neolithic period, and for the first two phases of the Chalcolithic, there is no trace at all of the earliest development of a temple-building culture, something that one might expect to find if this had had its roots in Malta itself. Both the rock-cut tombs—which, it has been plausibly suggested, inspired the original shapes of the temples—and the temples themselves only appear in the Ġgantija phase (although it is probable that the use of the tombs at Xemxija began at the end of the preceding Mġarr phase). It seems incredible that neither of these important and interlinked features of the advanced Maltese Chalcolithic culture appeared until such a late stage in the evolution of the islands' prehistoric society, and that the temples then rapidly underwent almost their entire architectural develop-

The sites of collective burial in Neolithic and Chalcolithic Europe.

ment in one phase, if no outside influences were involved. It is even more surprising since there now appears to be a substantial cultural gap between the Neolithic and Chalcolithic periods at about perhaps 4000 BC and it seems probable that some new stone-using agricultural people arrived on Malta at that time. The slow evolution of the temple-building culture would perhaps have begun then with the appearance in rudimentary form of the features (such as rock-cut tombs) which later became so important. Yet nothing appears until many centuries later.

The alternative hypothesis is that some newcomers—few in number perhaps but influential and perhaps with armed followers—came to Malta

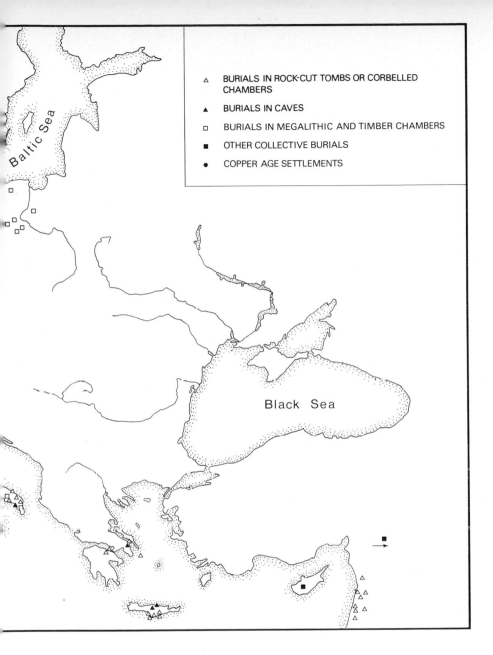

Baltic Sea

Black Sea

towards the end of the Mġarr phase, formed a new dominant class, introduced the new rite of collective burial for themselves in rock-cut graves (which they found could be made easily in the local soft limestone), intermarried with the local leading families and then embarked on a programme of influencing or coercing the local population to construct increasingly grandiose standing temples (modelled at first on the rock-tombs). One must admit that this seems at least as likely from the evidence as the alternative isolationist view. The onset of the period of use of the rock-cut tombs and of temple-building at such a relatively late stage in the islands' prehistory might be said to be the cultural equivalent of a biological mutation and surely requires an injection of new talent, and new men, from elsewhere to set it going.

It is interesting at this point to recall three opinions expressed by Professor Bernabó Brea in 1960, before work had started at Skorba and when no radiocarbon dates were available for Maltese prehistory.

To Professor Brea the pottery evidence indicated a substantial break between the earliest phase of human occupation on Malta and the next phase, then thought to be the Zebbug. Excavations at Skorba have since proved this view to be absolutely correct. Meanwhile, archaeological features of the final, Tarxien phase of the temple-building culture persuaded him that it was contemporary not with a second-millennium Mycenean culture, as Professor Evans thought, but with the Aegean Early Bronze Age in the third millennium. Radiocarbon dating later showed him to be right on this point too. Nor did Professor Brea agree that the rise of the temple-building culture was an entirely local phenomenon, unconnected with outside events.

He pointed out that such a dramatic cultural flowering would normally best be explained by an increase in maritime enterprise and trade among the advanced coastal peoples of the eastern Mediterranean and the Aegean. Malta and Gozo, being small, rocky and not too fertile, could never have supported a large agricultural population in Neolithic times and food would have had to be imported to support a temple-building civilization, especially one that was so active while it lasted. One cannot but wonder whether Professor Brea's judgement on the general problem of the origins of the temple culture was not as reliable as his views on its phases proved to be.

The appearance of the rite of collective burial on Malta may be the clue to the arrival of a new dominant group that is needed: no such graves are known from the earlier phases. A distinct burial rite—particularly one that seems so intimately linked with the priesthood and the temples, as is so clearly seen in the combination of the two traditions in the Tarxien hypogeum—can be as good a sign as any of the appearance of foreigners. It could be the kind of tradition which is retained as a cherished link with the abandoned homeland. Collective burial may itself have become popular because it symbolized the separateness and exclusiveness of the people concerned in their newly adopted lands and among their newly subjugated peoples. Perhaps the 7,000 or so individuals buried in the hypogeum, and the smaller numbers in the other rock-cut tombs, are the remains of some 30 successive generations of a new governing class and their associates. Examination of the other provinces of the megalith builders reveals that the one most important connecting thread linking them all is this rite of collective burial, always—where the evidence is available—introduced among an existing agricultural population whose funerary traditions are quite different and usually inaugurating a period of monument building.

In the light of the possibility that the people practising collective burial may have been members of an élite class it is particularly interesting to read the anatomist's reports on the human remains found in the rock-cut tombs at Xemxija, at St. Paul's Bay. Five tombs were found there and the contents make it clear that, though some may have been dug and used at the end of the Mġarr phase, the main period of the interments was the temple-building Ġgantija and Tarxien phases. A notable feature of the human bones found in the tombs was the absence of any deep grooves caused by the attachment of particularly strong muscles. The author noted: '. . . it seems probable that they did not engage in any manual labour. The last point is of particular interest, for if the inference is correct, it is possible that the Xemxija burials represented a special group or class rather than a cross-section of the population.'

Also relevant here may be the fact that a detailed examination of the teeth found in the tombs revealed evidence, first that some extractions may have been done during the lifetime of the individuals concerned and, second, that: 'The strikingly low incidence of marked attrition (tooth wear) would indicate a diet relatively free from fibrous and gritty particles. The caries found, as well as the number of teeth lost *ante mortem*, could be another indication.' In other words the people buried in these tombs evidently ate a diet free of coarse, rough food—another indication perhaps of social status.

The absence of much foreign influence on the pottery of the Mġarr and Ġgantija periods need only mean that the hypothetical newcomers were prepared or obliged to adopt the local wares (and patronize the local potters) which were in any case of very high quality: widely traded pottery did not in fact become common in the Mediterranean area until much later, in Mycenaean times. The ship carvings found in the Tarxien temples may be hinting too at the importance to the temple-building culture of overseas contacts. Neither is it necessary to assume that a sacred island with a prestigious temple attracting pilgrims from elsewhere must necessarily show a mass of imported archaeological material as part of this phenomenon; we do not normally take tea-sets with us to places of pilgrimage. However, support for the Maltese temples and their priests from outside the islands is not a necessary part of the hypothesis offered here: once it had been started by the new dominant class, the new stratified society with its professional castes could have been an entirely local phenomenon, particularly if—as seems likely—the islands were more wooded and fertile 5,000 years ago than they are now and could then have supported several thousand Neolithic peasant farmers.

The last points concern the dating of the Maltese sequence and the religion of the temple builders. Now that it is known that the Chalcolithic temple culture lasted from at least as early as 3500 BC until about 2500 BC, the megalithic traditions of Malta are seen to be contemporary with, not later than, those of mainland Europe, though they need not necessarily be older than them. Links between the later and most technically advanced megalith builders and those further west and north-west are quite possible. Links with the early Helladic period in the Aegean are also possible and similarities between the statue-menhirs of the Zebbug period and those of Troy have been recorded. However, if it is assumed that the temple culture

Evidence of collective burial in Neolithic and Chalcolithic Europe is largely found in the rock-cut tombs of the Mediterranean area and in artificial stone or wooden chambers inside built mounds in Iberia, France, Ireland, Britain, Scandinavia, north Germany and Poland. Palmela (top left) is one of a small group of outlying rock-cut tombs in Iberia. Camster Round in Scotland (below) is a chambered tomb under a mound. The tombs were opened and re-used over many generations, older bones sometimes being stacked up to make way for new interments. This contrasts with the habit in the succeeding Bronze Age when a body would more usually be put in an individual cist (left) and the mound left undisturbed afterwards. The builders of Europe's megalithic tombs are thus linked not only by the very practice of exploiting stone but by the custom of collective burial too.

Megalithic tombs as they stand today are often ghosts of their original appearance. Camster Round (opposite bottom) has retained its great covering cairn, and the interiors of some of the passage graves are still fully lintelled or at least have most of their uprights in place (right), but other tombs have entirely lost their protective mounds (below).

was inaugurated at about 3500 BC by a few skilled newcomers, the question arises where these could have come from at such an early date. Their arrival would have been well before the rise of the Early Bronze Age city-based cultures of the Aegean and before the unification of Egypt in about 3100 BC. The Sumerian city states of Mesopotamia were in existence by the middle of the fourth millennium BC according to the traditional chronology.

Of the form of religion practised by the priests of the megalithic temples of Malta little can be inferrred and the meagre evidence available suggests that it may have been of two kinds. A number of stylized clay figurines of enormously fat women have been found in the temples and strongly suggest the sort of age-old fertility cult that Neolithic peasants would surely demand that their priests administer for them. Both standing and squatting figures are known, some being painted red. There are also a few figurines which seem to show bodies deformed by illness and these may be examples of the sort of sympathetic magic which can still be seen, for example in Barcelona cathedral, in the form of wax images of parts of the human body. Portraits of the priests and priestesses themselves may be visible in another group of figurines showing partly clothed human forms.

On the other hand the horned facades of the temples, as well as the drawings of bulls at Tarxien, may indicate that a bull-god cult was the main religion of the priestly class. The bull is well known as the *alter ego* of Zeus/Jupiter, the Horus of the Egyptians or the Astarte of the Palestinians. Whether the red-painted rooms inside the temples were also connected with this cult is uncertain. One might hazard a guess that the Maltese temples were raised to a major deity of the ancient world like the equivalent of Zeus, or the earlier Cronos, and that the priests also performed less sophisticated fertility and other rites for the benefit of the aboriginal peasant population. The probability that a horned god cult was practised by the Maltese Chalcolithic priestly class between about 3500 and 2500 BC is increased by the frequency of the horned cairn throughout the megalithic province of western Europe at about this time.

The nine radiocarbon dates now available for the Neolithic and Chalcolithic phases of the islands' prehistory make it clear that the whole of the time that collective burial was practised and temples were built—the end of the Mġarr phase and the Ggantija and Tarxien phases—fell between about 3500 and 2500 BC. Thus the Maltese megalithic temple-builders, whatever their origins, probably played no part in the origin of megalith building in Atlantic Europe which seems to have begun at least a millennium earlier, at about 4500 BC. They might of course have influenced the latter— or been influenced by them—at a later stage.

Iberia

Except for a small area of southern France the Iberian peninsula is the only place in Europe where passage graves are associated with a technologically advanced, copper-using culture whose creators also built fortified settlements at a later stage.

A form of religion practised in the Maltese megalithic temples is not easy to infer from the evidence available. A number of clay models of stylized fat women have been found (above, below left) and at Tarxien a slab carved with two bulls and a sow with piglets (right). The figurines might suggest the sort of fertility cult that a Neolithic population would follow. The bulls may be linked with the horned facades of the temples to imply some kind of bull-god cult.

The quantity and quality of decorative carving at Tarxien (above, left) and Hagar Qim (below) in Malta suggest that the temple builders supported specialist crafts-men.

The major developments in Neolithic and Chalcolithic Iberia are slowly being clarified although many areas are still obscure as regards their dating and place in the overall sequence. The earliest Neolithic, or food-producing, peoples were evidently those using impressed Cardial ware and had appeared on the east coast of Spain before 5000 BC, bringing with them cultivated barley and domesticated animals. The foundations of a stable, settled village society—capable eventually of erecting impressive stone monuments and probably of supporting a small class of full-time religious and other specialists—should have been laid at this time, presumably through cultural and genetic mixing between newcomers and aborigines. The fact that communities of the native hunting and collecting peoples were still in Spain and Portugal at that time is shown by the dates for the Mesolithic sites at Muge on the coast of Portugal which overlap with the earliest Neolithic dates.

The middle Neolithic phase is marked by the appearance of open villages whose inhabitants had quernstones, polished stone axes, long flint blades, simple undecorated pottery bowls and geometric flint microliths. These last show that the earliest farming peoples had mixed with the aboriginal hunting communities—perhaps by intermarriage—and had produced a new hybrid population which inherited skills from both groups.

The existence of collective burial is attested at some stage in the later Neolithic period in south-eastern Spain but no exact dates are yet available. By contrast, collective burial in simple megalithic passage graves seems to be confirmed for the fifth millennium BC in Portugal and—as in Malta—there seems to be a link between the appearance of this funerary rite and the start of the construction of a long series of increasingly elaborate stone monuments.

Although there are differences in detail between the Almerian Neolithic culture of south-east Spain and the corresponding culture of Portugal and the west, the evolution of the passage graves seems to have followed broadly similar lines in both areas. The oldest forms were the simple megalithic constructions (*antas* in Portugal) but these were succeeded by more sophisticated buildings which seem to have had beehive domes of drystone walling covering the chambers. In Portugal the appearance of this new kind of passage grave seems to inaugurate the late Neolithic period in which the earliest copper implements appear. The new phase there is marked also by the appearance of novel items like slate plaques with incised decoration in geometrical patterns, flint arrowheads with a concave base and ground-stone axes with a rectangular instead of a round cross-section. In the rock-cut tombs of the Tagus estuary appear many stone 'cult objects', perhaps used in funerary ceremonies, as well as the groove-decorated 'import ware' and the pattern-burnished wares.

Many of the late Neolithic and Chalcolithic features of western Iberia are also seen in the south-east, particularly at the great settlement site of Los Millares. The sheer size of this settlement is also unmatched in the west and suggests that Los Millares was an important small Chalcolithic town the influences from which were felt all through the coastal provinces.

The evolution of the Iberian passage graves seems to have progressed towards greater size and increasing complexity with a relatively late tomb like the Cueva del Romeral at Antequera having a very long passage and a side-chamber opening off the main one. Such side-chambers are seen quite often at Los Millares together with other embellishments like port-hole slabs set into the entrance passages. One or two tombs elsewhere are known to have had a stone basin in the burial chamber, a feature which is encountered again in Ireland.

Beaker pottery is consistently found with the latest burials in Iberian passage graves and rock-cut tombs—occurring in particularly large quantities on the Tagus estuary sites—and the many radiocarbon dates for Beaker period sites in Iberia and elsewhere suggest that the influence of these people increased rapidly at around 2500 BC. The decline and abandonment of some of the Chalcolithic castros seems to have occurred at this time and it marks a convenient point at which to end the Copper Age and begin the Early Bronze Age. The new TL dates seem to show that collective burial in megalithic passage graves in Iberia goes back to at least as early as 4000 BC, and probably to the middle of the fifth millennium, long before the emergence of the Chalcolithic settlements.

The archaeology of Neolithic and Chalcolithic Iberia thus suggests that something similar happened in Spain and Portugal as can be seen to have occurred in Malta a few centuries later. At the beginning of Neolithic times—well before 5000 BC—the population seems to have been composed of simple farmers and herdsmen, the little evidence of burials available suggesting that they practised individual interments. Then some centuries, or perhaps a millennium or more, after this first Neolithic colonization the first collective monumental tombs appear.

The emergence of the rite of collective burial almost certainly means that a new class of dominant people had arrived or developed in Iberia. Even though at first their grave goods are simple Neolithic articles, what happened later seems to confirm that they were a class apart, as also does the existence of the massive tombs themselves, requiring a very large outlay of effort to plan and build. The later tombs have richer and much more varied grave goods and, unless one assumes that the whole population increased in wealth at a uniform rate, this does suggest that one group was steadily increasing in wealth and influence.

In fact the unique evidence from Los Millares shows very convincingly that this was so and provides the vital clue to the nature of the passage grave builders which is lacking from all other regions in which they were set up. This site provides a direct and invaluable link between the large and architecturally sophisticated late passage graves—descended from earlier, simpler ones on the same site—and the highly organized Chalcolithic walled settlement with its outer redoubts and its abundant evidence of metallurgy and other specialized activities of town life. There can be little doubt that here it was not the ordinary rural population which was buried inside these great constructions but members of the governing and dominant classes of

The ditched enclosure and stone circle at Brogar on Orkney. ▶

the flourishing proto-urban settlement. The old view that the Copper Age settlements were built by intrusive colonists has been rightly rejected by Renfrew for a variety of reasons (although we might offer the suggestion that new rulers, with professional warriors, may have taken over at around 3000 BC, or whenever the bastioned fortifications were built). It is now becoming clear that these settlements were the products of a society or a class which had evolved from beginnings in the fifth millennium BC and whose members were buried collectively in monumental tombs. The Iberian evidence thus seems to be pointing clearly to the conclusion that collective burial nearly everywhere—especially in architecturally impressive buildings—was the practice of one or more specialized upper classes. The Maltese evidence and that from the megalith builders of north-west Europe suggests that this class was a theocratic one, though in Iberia it is possible that the tombs held a broader segment of the non-farming population.

This last point tends to be emphasized by some recent suggestions by A. Gilman and others that irrigation may have played an important part in the rise of a stratified society in south-east Spain in Neolithic and Chalcolithic times and its subsequent development into a militaristic one in the Early Bronze Age. Evidence for the design and construction of an agricultural system based on water channels is still sparse but, if confirmed, will tend to reinforce the idea that a well-organized governing class served by specialist professions was present in Iberia in the fourth and third millennia BC.

Thus, in general, the appearance and development of the rite of collective burial in Iberia seems well explained in evolutionary (as opposed to Lamarckian) terms—a specialized group of people, probably not farmers, arrived in the country, or separated out there, and became successful, steadily increasing in prestige, influence and wealth in the main trading centres and sending out offshoots to, and promoting imitators in, the poorer hinterlands round about. The various archaeological links which have been detected with Italian, east Mediterranean and north African Neolithic and Early Bronze Age cultures raise the question of whether the earliest of these people were actual immigrant specialists from the east or from North Africa, or a combination of the two. Does this lead on to any conclusions about the origin of the passage grave builders and of the rite of collective burial itself?

The crucial fact is that the characteristic collective stone tombs of western and south-western Atlantic Europe are passage graves, mainly built above ground but occasionally rock-cut, and that these seem not to be known anywhere further east in the fifth millennium BC. The implication is that this tomb-type was invented in Iberia, perhaps as a unique local combination of an imported idea and a local tradition. Neither must it be forgotten, when considering the problem of origins, that the megalithic buildings could have been temples as well as tombs and could thus demonstrate the appearance of an important religious cult.

One could argue plausibly that both the rite of collective burial itself and the passage grave megalithic temple-tomb were Iberian Neolithic developments (though there is still a possibility that the burial rite came from further east). The people who built and used the tombs could also have been a local development, in the sense of being hybrids between two distinct groups—for example north Africans and people from the eastern Mediterranean. The evidence of physical anthropology, meagre though it is, suggests that the Iberian chambered tomb population might have been a blend of such east Mediterranean and north African forms. As a working hypothesis it may be suggested that this is in fact what happened and that a stratified, perhaps theocratic society began to emerge in Spain and Portugal in the fifth millennium BC as the result of the superposition of skilled dominant groups of varying origins on a substratum of Neolithic farmers. The great megalithic monuments would then be the visible sign that this had happened and would bear witness to the creativity and energy of this new dominant class.

Finally, the advent of the new TL dates for Iberian collective tombs has disposed, at least temporarily, of two explanations for the origin of the European megalithic chambered mounds. In the first place it is difficult to argue now that the collective tombs of Chalcolithic Malta mark a stage in the westward movement of people bearing this rite along the Mediterranean sea. At present, the earliest temples and tombs on Malta seem to be many centuries later than those of Iberia. In the second place it is no longer possible to deny the northward spread of collective burial and passage graves from Iberia simply because the great cairns of Brittany were the oldest known. Those in Portugal are at least as old so an Iberian origin, favoured by all the other evidence, is now favoured also by the available dates.

France

The spread of relatively standardized passage graves across Europe includes two compact groups in France which are close to Iberia—one in the south-east overlooking the Golfe du Lion and the other in Brittany in the north-west. The sea routes from Iberia are short and direct and indeed any northward sailing ships from northern Spain could hardly fail to see the Breton peninsula once across the Bay of Biscay. Both these groups of French passage graves are close to the coast and have such an obvious sea link with Iberia that very strong reasons would be needed to reject the notion that they represent the transfer of the idea of the passage grave, and of collective burial, from one region to the other.

The only alternative to this view is to assume that the passage graves were the result of spontaneous and independent local developments in megalithic architecture which took similar forms for reasons which are not usually specified too clearly—presumably through trading and 'influences'. This theory makes some very large assumptions about human nature. Professor Renfrew has argued the case in some detail but there is an alternative hypothesis that might fit the facts as well or better. This is the one most recently advocated by C. D. Darlington and envisages the megalith builders as a stable caste of professional priests and wise men who settled among, and came to dominate, the Neolithic peasant populations of Atlantic Europe.

Primitive farmers were in southern France at a very early date, long before any megaliths could have been built. But so few settlement sites have yet been radiocarbon-dated in Brittany that it is not known whether Neolithic agriculturalists or herdsmen were in that part of the country for any length of time before the start of megalith building.

A plausible sequence of megalithic cairns and pottery in Brittany has been worked out by Giot and L'Helgouach. Even though there are still no radiocarbon dates for the gallery graves so that we cannot be sure that some of them are not as old as the earliest passage graves, it seems clear that the earliest megalithic constructions are the simplest or 'classic' passage graves of early Iberian type and that these later developed into several local varieties. It is difficult to deny that this is exactly what one would expect if the idea of the passage grave were brought to Brittany in the mid-fifth millennium BC from Iberia and took root and flourished for many centuries. The coastal distribution of the passage graves and the peculiar geographical position of Brittany in relation to Iberia and the Atlantic sea-lanes all favour this view. Radiocarbon dates confirm that the earliest megalithic constructions of Brittany were being built around 4500 BC.

When Colin Renfrew discussed these early Breton dates no radio-carbon dates remotely comparable were known from Iberian megaliths and he was able confidently to assert that the clear priority of Brittany in the passage grave tradition made nonsense of the view that these structures were taken northwards from Spain and Portugal. The argument seemed a strong one and helped to prop up a formidable case in favour of the independent European development of the graves. The alternative hypothesis must inevitably doubt that this could have occurred, especially as the later passage graves of Iberia are now associated with advanced metal-using cultures which were technologically far more sophisticated than anything of the same period further north in Atlantic Europe. It cannot be a surprise then to someone taking a Darwinian view that the new TL dates from the Iberian passage graves reveal that the megaliths there were also flourishing in the middle of the fifth millennium BC. There is no reason to doubt, therefore, what the distribution and design of the passage graves suggests, that they were devised first in Iberia and that the idea of them was transported north-east to southern France and northwards across the Bay of Biscay to Brittany by migrants of some kind.

The Breton passage graves evolve, as would be expected, from the primary, simple forms through several local varieties until finally, in late Neolithic times, appear the gallery graves with their links with the long mounds of Britain and northern Europe. The oldest of the true long barrow collective graves seem to be those of south-eastern England which appear as early as about 4000 BC, and the megalithic versions of Atlantic Britain may be almost as early. If this is so, the appearance of long mounds in Brittany and northern Europe may reflect the outward, return spread of the idea from

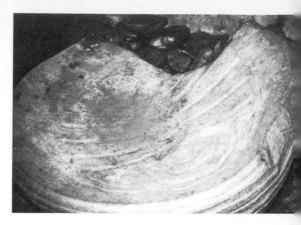

A stone basin found in the megalithic passage grave at Knowth in Ireland (left, above) forges an early 3rd millennium link with Portugal where similar basins have been found in collective tombs. Pecked abstract patterns on the Knowth stones (below) are matched in the Breton tombs.

Britain, centuries after the passage grave and the idea of collective burial had arrived in the north. This view must, in turn, be reconsidered if the long cairns of Brittany which enclose passage graves—like Barnenez, Île Gaignog, Fontenay le Marmion and Er Rohec—are Breton versions of the general long-cairn tradition, forming 'hybrid' cairns. The early date of Barnenez would then mean that the long-cairn tradition was in existence as early as 4500 BC and was as old as the passage graves. Since these cairns have no plausible prototypes in Iberia, they might represent an independent European development of the rite of collective burial. However, it seems possible to take, with Dr John Corcoran, the view that the Breton cairns mentioned are a local device, designed to accommodate several passage graves inside a cairn with the least effort, and quite distinct from the later true long-cairn tradition. In the latter the mound is far larger than it needs to be to enclose the burial chamber.

Ireland

The Irish megaliths pose the same problem as those in Britain: were they introduced to a pre-existing Neolithic agricultural population or were they brought over by the first immigrant farmers? Since most early Neolithic radiocarbon dates come from the collective tombs themselves—and since, without the hypothesis of a Neolithic priestly caste, the problem does not really arise—it is perhaps not surprising that the question does not seem to have perturbed anyone recently. Yet it is a vital one since one would expect a priestly caste, unless it actually organized the Neolithic settlement, to arrive only after a farming population had been well established and could be expected to support a specialized group of people contributing nothing to food production.

The oldest collective tombs in Britain so far known go back to a little before 4000 BC. In England the only other signs of Neolithic activity as early as that are seen in the flint mines at Church Hill in Sussex (3390 ± 150 bc) and the causewayed camp at Hembury, Devon (oldest date at 3330 ± 150 bc). The majority of barrows, camps, flint mines and occupation sites fall in the following centuries, reinforcing the impression that the collective tombs came with the first farming colonists. This helps the idea that the funerary monuments were set up for the ordinary rural farming population and have no special significance in terms of professional priesthoods.

However, discoveries in recent years at Ballynagilly in Co. Tyrone seem to show that this impression is quite wrong. A long series of radiocarbon dates has been obtained from a Neolithic occupation site, now under peat, on which there are traces of pits and houses associated with early Neolithic pottery and other artefacts. No less than three of these dates fell before 3600 bc, one being 3795 ± 90 bc. It seems clear, therefore, that the first agriculturalists were in Ireland by soon after 4500 BC—when the first passage graves were being built in Brittany—and that the collective burial people may indeed have come to these islands centuries after their colonization by farmers.

165

T. G. E. Powell made the same point in 1969, using slightly different evidence. Traces of the first large-scale colonization of the British Isles by Neolithic farmers is seen in the record of ancient vegetation preserved as fossil pollen. Their 'land-taking' is detectable in a sharp decline in elm pollen and a rise in that of weeds flourishing in open conditions. Occasionally the pollen grains of cultivated cereals are identified at the same level. The assumption is that the elm decline was due to the felling of the forests all over north-western Europe by the first Neolithic colonists. Radiocarbon dates for this level in the pollen deposits fall between about 3400 and 3100 bc (about 4100 and 3800 BC) and are close to the date of the oldest collective graves under long barrows. However, the Ballynagilly evidence seems to confirm that the first farmers did arrive a few centuries before the first collective tombs were built so that the latter could have been introduced to an already settled population. A land-taking was in fact identified at the Irish site and carbon-dated to about 3800 BC.

Although very few of the Irish passage graves have been accurately dated by radiocarbon it does seem clear that the large and elaborate 'Boyne' tombs belong mainly to the first half of the third millennium BC and are all younger than about 3200 BC. Some, such as Tara, and perhaps Knowth, may have been built only a short while before the arrival of the Beaker people at about 2500 BC. Nevertheless, the much smaller satellite passage graves at Knowth do seem to be earlier than the main mound and suggest that the large 'Boyne' tombs were added to pre-existing cemeteries. Evidently the Irish passage graves evolved like those in Iberia and Brittany—the earliest being small, with relatively short passages, and the later ones more elaborate, sometimes with side chambers, and tending to have longer passages.

Other links between Ireland and Portugal during the period of the Millaran culture (c. 3000–2500 BC) include bone pins found in the tombs in both areas and stone basins. Further links between the British Isles and Portugal are apparent in some features of tomb decoration—such as 'serpentiform' motifs—but the second great period of megalith building gives the clearest impression of the arrival of skilled men from Iberia.

Britain

In contrast with Ireland the collective Neolithic tombs of Britain—both the chambered and unchambered kinds—have produced many useful radiocarbon dates as well as large numbers of human remains and associated artefacts. But for what part of the Neolithic society of the fourth and third millennia BC were they built? There are in fact some other early Neolithic graves, besides those under the long barrows and cairns, that are relatively humble interments and cannot be interpreted as collective tombs. In view of the indications from Malta and Iberia that collective burial was practised by an upper class—and the same strong suggestion given by the sophisticated nature of the best of the megalithic tombs from Atlantic Europe and the British Isles—this meagre evidence could be of great importance. I maintain

Pottery of the megalith building period in Britain is of a plain kind like that from the early 4th millennium mortuary structure at Fussell's Lodge (above) or groove-decorated ware that has now been found both at the ceremonial centres of southern England, including mid-3rd millennium Durrington Walls (top right), and in Orkney. A little drum of chalk bears the same geometrical patterns as the grooved pots and 'eye-brows' like those seen on some Iberian pottery of the early 3rd millennium. A long-headed skull from a cairn in Scotland is characteristic of all those yet found in the collective graves and is in contrast with the round-headed type of the succeeding Bronze Age (below left and right).

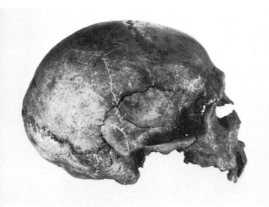

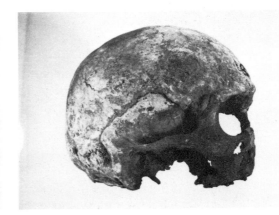

that the people who lived temporarily in Neolithic causewayed camps like Windmill Hill were very probably of ordinary peasant stock and that they contrasted sharply in their dietary habits with the inhabitants of the nearby late Neolithic ditched ceremonial enclosures with their massive wooden buildings. It seems reasonable to conclude that these humble individual burials in the causewayed camps represent the funerary habits of the ordinary rural population. Likewise, the graves at Cissbury and Blackpatch were probably simply those of flint miners and their families. Again the contrast with the massive collective tombs is striking and it is difficult not to conclude that in Britain also the latter were for a very special group of people.

The hypothesis that the great barrows and cairns were the burial mounds of whole Neolithic communities was never tenable once it had been shown that the period concerned lasted much longer than two centuries or so. Now that two millennia, perhaps more, are known to have been involved, it is simply not possible to believe that the few hundred individuals found in the chambered cairns and long barrows in Britain and Ireland were other than a very select group.

The ethnic type of the skulls found in the collective graves can be interpreted as supporting this view. The skulls themselves do not indicate whether they are the remains of a stable priestly caste or of a random collection of peasants of similar physical type but the close racial similarity between the dolichocephalic people buried in the long barrows of southern England and the chambered cairns of Scotland fits exactly with the concept that they were all a related upper class of Iberian origin. It is a pity that there seems to be no up-to-date physical anthropological study of the human remains from the Iberian collective tombs.

However, it remains true that the almost complete absence of a different set of more humble Neolithic graves, particularly in Scotland, deprives us of the necessary comparative evidence which would test the caste theory properly.

Regional variations apart, the material culture of early Neolithic Britain is remarkably uniform and it must be accepted that, if there was a stratified society existing then with an upper class supported by the rest, it is not obvious from the pottery and artefacts but only from the buildings. One exception might be the Unstan pottery, the finely decorated version of the universal Neolithic round-based bowls which is found in Orkney and Caithness. This comparative uniformity in the material culture would be a strong point to stress in a non-diffusionist view of the Neolithic cairns—and in an egalitarian view of the societies which built them. Not until late Neolithic times does evidence from the pottery, artefacts and animal bones indicate at all clearly that a stratified society, including a supported upper class, was in existence. The cairns themselves provide the only evidence for this in earlier times.

Several facts seem to stand out about the nature, origins and evolution of the collective tombs and their builders in Britain and Ireland from the assembled evidence. In the first place, there is the well-dated arrival, at about 4200 BC, of an entirely new kind of people practising collective burial—using wooden mortuary structures and burying these under long mounds. It seems possible that these represent the arrival of a strong eastern European tradition since wedge-shaped wooden Neolithic long houses of similar dimensions are known from Poland and eastern Germany. Some well-preserved examples of the barrows, like Pimperne in Dorset, have a clear ridge along the spine, like the ridge of a roof, and excavation has revealed traces of upright wooden walls in some. On the other hand it has been suggested by Jażdżewski that the long barrow collective burial tradition originated in England, where the oldest ones seem to be, and spread from there to the continent of Europe.

The pottery from eastern England also has links with the early Neolithic wares in Denmark and north-eastern Europe, particularly in the shoulder often found on the round-based bowls there. If collective burial was ultimately brought to the north from Iberia by groups of special and influential people then these would have to have arrived in Britain or northern Europe, and created there a special local version of their élite culture, well back in the fifth millennium BC. Only in this way could this northern long barrow culture have appeared fully formed in south-east England soon after 4000 BC. Alternatively, the barrow culture may have been a purely northern phenomenon with diverse origins and there may be no case for the southern derivation of collective burial.

Dates from the Monamore cairn and from the Lochhill long cairn in Scotland show that the horned, megalithic cairns were also in existence soon after 4000 BC in south-west Scotland and probably in the Severn-Cotswold region also. These were doubtless a blend of the long-barrow traditions and those of the earliest megaliths already in the west (portal dolmens, primitive small passage graves and 'protomegaliths') and they must clearly show that these megaliths were also established before 4000 BC, perhaps well before. The fact that each group of cairns tends to have characteristic and consistent local features—transepted galleries around the Severn, segmented chambers in Argyll and all the strange forms in the far north—shows well that several small groups arrived at a very early date, that they established themselves and that each created a hybrid, local religious culture which, being successful, multiplied and expanded in area over the following centuries. However, the possibility must not be ignored that the practice of using megalithic blocks occasionally did arise spontaneously in northern Europe. Early Neolithic stone tombs in Denmark, known as *dysser*, may be an example; though, since they seem to date to not earlier than the fourth millennium BC, influence from other megalith builders cannot be ruled out.

Although the passage graves are really common only in the far north and north-west, there are strong suspicions that simple ones appeared at a very early date in other regions also but did not survive there the impact of the beliefs of the long-barrow builders. This situation is quite compatible with the early spread of passage-grave builders from Iberia or Brittany to

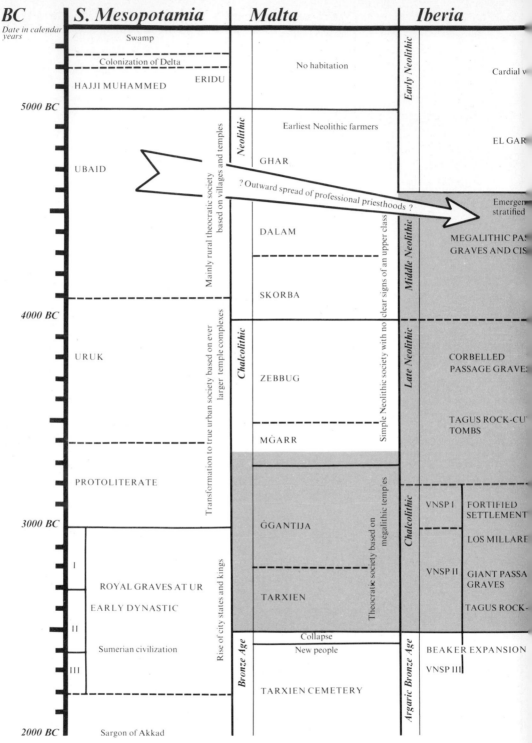

When, and in what social context collective burial (shaded) and megalith building occurred in Mediterranean and Atlantic Europe. VNSP = Vila Nova de São Pedro.

170

	Brittany		Ireland		England/Scotland
		Mesolithic		*Mesolithic*	
	Not known if farmers here already				
			Scattered bands of hunters		Scattered bands of hunters
Early and Middle Neolithic	EARLIEST PASSAGE GRAVES MEGALITHIC PASSAGE GRAVES AND CISTS	*Neolithic*	First traces of farmers		
			HORNED LONG CHAMBERED CAIRNS	*Early Neolithic*	First traces of farmers LONG BARROWS AND LONG CHAMBERED CAIRNS SOME SMALL PASSAGE GRAVES IN WEST AND NORTH
	LOCAL FORMS OF PASSAGE GRAVES DEVELOP		PRESUMABLY SOME EARLY SMALL PASSAGE GRAVES		
			COURT CAIRNS		QUANTERNESS
Late Neolithic	DECORATED MEGALITHS LONG GALLERY GRAVES LATE LOCAL FORMS OF PASSAGE GRAVES, INCLUDING LARGE ONES		NEW GRANGE DECORATED MEGALITHS GIANT PASSAGE GRAVES (NEW GRANGE, KNOWTH) MEGALITHIC ALIGNMENTS	*Middle Neolithic*	SKARA BRAE I CLAVA CAIRNS STONEHENGE I SILBURY HILL EARLY STONE CIRCLES ELABORATE ORKNEY PASSAGE GRAVES
Bronze Age	BEAKER EXPANSION	*Bronze Age*	BEAKER EXPANSION	*Late Neolithic / Chalcolithic*	SKARA BRAE II DURRINGTON WALLS STANDING STONES AND STONE CIRCLES BEAKERS STONEHENGE II STONEHENGE III CUP AND RING CARVINGS

Rise of astronomy-practising theocracy

Ireland and parts of western Britain in the fifth millennium BC although there are still no Neolithic radiocarbon dates as early as that except from the settlement at Ballynagilly in Ulster. Indeed the evidence for early small passage graves in Britain, provided by the accurate dating of the arrival of the long mounds which covered some of them, goes far to support an Iberian origin for the type. All the later regional developments in collective tombs could be reasonably explained as local sects of theocrats establishing themselves, forming local hybrid collective tomb cultures and steadily improving their monumental architecture as far as local talent and building resources allowed. In this view the finest tombs on the Boyne, in Orkney, Caithness and elsewhere would be the parallel but largely independent northern flowerings of a variety of stratified, well organized societies with similar origins—all ultimately stemming from the arrival of élite specialist groups from outside, to settle among and 'exploit' or 'serve'—depending on one's viewpoint—an established rural population of peasant farmers.

In this view some of the local collective tomb 'sects' had greater success in their temple architecture than others but all were perhaps supported by the agricultural population with food and labour, all were buried as a race or class apart in their monumental tombs and all used local pottery and equipment. There is very little evidence of the ordinary farming people—not much more than a few graves, scatters of pottery and finds on some open sites and traces of fire and cultivation in ancient bog deposits. Certain of the hypothetical élite groups seem, however, to have set off down the path of intellectual advancement in spheres other than architecture and these, it seems, were the ones who had great success at the end of the Neolithic period.

Chapter XI The Megalith Builders

That professional priesthoods existed in north-west Europe in the middle of the third millennium BC, and were almost certainly descended from the passage grave builders of earlier times, is abundantly testified to by the stone circles and the inhabited earthworks and stone villages of late Neolithic Britain. Indeed this evidence is of fundamental importance to an understanding of the kind of people the megalith builders were and of the kind of society that constructed the great barrows and cairns with their collective graves.

A mass of evidence has been collected over the past forty years which leaves little doubt that many, if not most of the stone circles and standing stones of Britain and Brittany were—in addition presumably to being temples of some kind—sophisticated and accurate astronomical observing instruments. And Professor Thom has shown that there was a considerable body of what may broadly be called 'scientific' as well as engineering knowledge available to some people in north-western Europe towards the end of the tomb-building period. Moreover, the territory where this knowledge flourished is far from Iberia, the probable home of the passage grave builders, and really remote from the earliest civilizations of the ancient Near East. If, with independent evidence, the existence of a professional priesthood in these remote regions at this time can be demonstrated, the existence of the institution in the passage grave period becomes more likely.

However, Thom has not gone unchallenged by the archaeological world. His conclusion that there was a highly skilled class of professional astronomer priests and wise men in existence when the standing stones were built simply does not fit with the picture of late Neolithic Britain which has been built up over many decades by many hands and from a great variety of archaeological evidence. This was a picture of a relatively simple society, barbarian and rural, probably with chiefs and a ruling hierarchy of some kind but with no sign of the sophisticated, semi-civilized priesthood that Thom's work should imply. The analogy preferred by many is with the Polynesian island chiefdoms as they existed until the nineteenth century.

It was with the aim of providing a solution to this apparent *impasse*—and one, moreover, which did not ignore or reject quantities of 'unpalatable' evidence—that I took up the problem in 1973. I tried to show that the apparent conflict between Thom's evidence and traditional archaeological theory could be illusory and that the picture of a primitive tribal society in late Neolithic Britain which is currently favoured is not the only one which can be built up on the hard archaeological evidence. Bearing in mind that theories about prehistoric societies cannot be derived directly from the archaeological evidence but must come largely from *analogies* drawn with recorded peoples with apparently similar economies and technologies, the traditional picture of late Neolithic British society can have no weight by itself if faced with an alternative which explains all the evidence as well or better.

A quite different kind of stratified Neolithic society can be postulated, similar to that of the ancient Maya people of central America, in which a small élite class of professional priests, wise men and rulers was supported with tribute and taxes by a predominantly rural peasant population. Such a society could have achieved all that Thom has suggested it did because the members of the élite would have been free from the need to obtain their own food and build their own dwellings and could have devoted their entire time to religious, scientific or other intellectual pursuits.

However, to suggest that there was such a stratified society in Britain at around 2500 BC we would have to be able to identify the residential centres where these supposed specialist élite classes lived and show, from the archaeological material found in these, that the occupants enjoyed a higher and more civilized standard of living than the rest of the population.

Way of life at Skara Brae

The finds made in the stone village of Skara Brae in the Orkneys are usually interpreted in terms of an isolated local community having few if any foreign contacts. However, not only does some Iberian pottery have very similar features to the Grooved ware from Skara Brae but there is another group of artefacts from the site which should be reconsidered with overseas influence in mind. These are strange stone artefacts—including a decorated three-spiked object, stone hatchets, a mushroom-shaped implement and carved stone balls. Nothing like them has been recorded anywhere else in Neolithic Britain and until now they have been thought to show that the people of Skara Brae included persons of very ancient Baltic or Scandinavian Mesolithic lineage, that is of some of the aborigines who may have been living nearby in scattered bands when the first Neolithic farmers arrived. Professor Childe drew some interesting comparisons between these objects and the stone implements of the 'Arctic Stone Age' cultures in those northern regions where farming was impossible and where the ancient hunting mode of life had survived late, even—as with the Eskimos and Lapps—down to modern times. It had long been believed that traces of Arctic Stone Age peoples survived late in northern Scotland and the curious implements from Skara Brae seemed to confirm this.

Yet in fact the graves of the Chalcolithic cultures of Iberia—in particular the rock-cut tombs of central Portugal—provide us with strange stone objects which are just as close to those of Skara Brae as the Arctic Stone Age ones. They have the advantage moreover of being approximately the same age as those of the Orkney site, of being found in a homogeneous context (unlike the 'Arctic' objects) and of having often been found with pottery and bone pins which find equally good analogies in the site in the Bay of Skaill. It is clear now that the more one examines the Orcadian site the more difficult it becomes to subscribe to the theory that it is of no more than local significance. In fact we shall eventually have to conclude that, far from being this, Skara Brae is a site of continental significance and provides us with the crucial evidence round which our understanding of the whole phenomenon of the megalith builders of Atlantic Europe may well have to pivot to face an entirely new direction.

In the main village deposits at Skara Brae—in the surrounding middens and on the hut floors—the bones of sheep and cattle were, according to Childe's excavation report, 'astoundingly numerous' and hardly any pig or deer bones were found there. A large proportion of the cattle bones were of immature beasts, and the explanation suggested was that autumn slaughtering was carried out (a practice due to the difficulty in some primitive environments of feeding stock through the winter). Huge quantities of shellfish were also eaten. By contrast the post-destruction deposits in Hut 7 gave only shells and bones of deer: the sheep and cattle seem to have vanished entirely. It was thus at first thought that the villagers did not grow any crops, but the latest excavations have revealed grains of barley at the base of the midden. Now the various stone mortars and pounders that have been found can be more convincingly thought to have been used for preparing cereals. In fact the new excavations are providing other new clues to the domestic economy of Skara Brae and until they are all published suggestions about the villagers' diet remain tentative.

Until recently there was no adequate means of comparing the diet of the people of Skara Brae with that of any other prehistoric communities in a similar environment and the assumption that their food was that of a normal peasant community hardly needed to be stated, let alone disputed. Now, however, we have detailed evidence of the animals eaten over a period of nearly a thousand years at Dun Mor Vaul, a Late Bronze and Iron Age site on Tiree in the Western Isles. This shows that, whenever the midden of an ordinary farming group was analysed—a group growing cereals and herding animals—about half their meat came from domestic animals (sheep and cattle) and half from game (red and roe deer and some birds). Although occupation of this site started some 2,000 years after Skara Brae was abandoned, and is over 320 kilometres to the south-west of Orkney, it seems reasonable to compare it with the Orcadian site because it is in an essentially similar Atlantic Scottish environment. Contemporary Neolithic and Iron Age sites of southern England show quite different proportions of animal bones—notably far fewer sheep and many more pigs—and this is obviously connected with the different climate and terrain in the south.

The contrast between the dietary habits of the people of Dun Mor Vaul and of Skara Brae itself suggests a social explanation which is supported by many other aspects of the Orkney site—that the inhabitants of Skara Brae were not peasants at all but some kind of élite group which was supported by gifts or tributes of food from the local rural population. The very high proportion of sheep and cattle in the main village middens, and the corresponding absence of deer bones, contrasts with the Tiree Iron Age site where half the meat eaten was game. However, one deposit at Dun Mor Vaul was very unusual; it was found in a chamber in the broch wall and was evidently the clayey midden-floor deposit of someone who had been living on the site while the broch was being constructed. He may have been the professional broch builder in charge of the project, being supplied with meat, bread and pottery by the local chief. A study of the masses of bones jammed into the floor of this cell—which was also crammed with potsherds—revealed a striking contrast with the other domestic deposits on the site. The bones of sheep and cattle were astonishingly numerous, totalling well over 90% of the whole collection: sheep bones were by far the commonest found.

If the evidence from the new excavations confirms the picture of the diet of the inhabitants of Skara Brae given by the work of Childe it will seem from this interesting side-light on an Iron Age professional fort-builder that the inhabitants of Skara Brae too were non-farming specialists, supplied with food produced by other people. Investigation of the related large ceremonial monuments of southern England has revealed a very similar situation there.

Other aspects of Skara Brae seem to match this supposition. In the first place there is the absolute uniqueness of the settlement: apart from the contemporary and related village of Rinyo and the earlier Neolithic house at Knap at Howar on Papa Westray, there is nothing like it anywhere else in northern Europe. The buildings are commodious and well designed by prehistoric and even recent rural standards; the existence of privies with drains is surely unmatched at that time outside contemporary Minoan Crete. The curious features of Hut 7—turning it into what might be a supervised place of confinement—could be well explained if the chamber were for vigils or concentrated study for the novices of some holy or learned order and the carvings on the bed slab could easily fit such a scheme by being interpreted as a tally of passing days.

The features of Hut 8 suggest a communal kitchen and work-room for the entire community—rather like the kitchens of medieval monasteries thousands of years later—where the imported meat and grain was prepared and cooked. The actual meals seem to have been taken in the separate huts or outside, a fact indicated by the distribution of discarded animal bones and by the lack of any midden around Hut 8 itself.

Even the nature of the happenings which followed the storm disaster could favour this view. The failure to clear 0·9 metres of sand from out of the structurally intact Hut 7 and to put a new roof on it would be understandable if the occupants of the village were a learned group unused

The furnishings of Hut 8 at Skara Brae are not like those of the other huts and suggest that it was a communal kitchen.

to such tasks while the complete disappearance of mutton and beef after the storm suggests the sudden cessation of tribute. It is rather hard to believe that a community of sturdy peasants would vanish so completely after such a disaster but if the village were a centrally organized community of learned and religious men with a special kitchen and workshop staff and an arrangement with the surrounding population for supplies the impoverishment of the inhabitants after the storm, or whatever it was, might be more easily visualized. Finally, the undoubtedly close connection between the pottery of Skara Brae and that found in the great ceremonial centres of southern England—as well as the possible links with the Irish passage graves and with Chalcolithic Portugal—could all argue quite strongly that the inhabitants of Skara Brae, far from being simple farmers eking out a 'miserable existence on a sea coast' as Professor Childe thought, were a very special group. Related sites in southern England, the great inhabited earthworks explored in the late 1960s and early 1970s by Geoffrey Wainwright, provide confirming evidence.

Temple, village or monastery at Durrington Walls?

Evidence gained from the large-scale excavations at Durrington Walls in Wiltshire suggested a conflict between the 'ritual' nature of the earthwork enclosure itself—apparently in the henge monument class—and the domestic-looking rubbish which was found in quantity inside it. Henge sites are not supposed to be inhabited and all previously explored examples were easily interpreted as temples or purely ceremonial sites of some kind. Yet the permanent habitation at Durrington Walls is quite a straightforward notion once this preconceived idea has been abandoned. Ash and other refuse tossed into the ditch terminal is better explained as domestic rubbish and waste dropped into a convenient deep pit a few yards from a large inhabited roundhouse than as 'ritual' offerings of some kind made by people entering or leaving a sacred precinct. The various other features deduced to be ceremonial or ritual are all just as easily explained in terms of a site which was lived in permanently by a community of some kind. If the earthwork enclosed a settlement which was a Neolithic combination of a monastery and a training college, one would expect there to be specially large communal buildings—even temples—for special purposes.

The question of the higher social status of the inhabitants of Durrington is really largely answered by the enormous amount of work which must have been put into the construction of the site in the mid-third millennium BC. The construction of the bank and ditch alone was a massive undertaking for a rural people, especially for one with a stone-using technology, and the equipment needed—thousands of red deer antlers for picks and hundreds of bovine shoulder blades for shovels as well as countless baskets—must have needed considerable organization. For example, the forests of England would have to have been systematically searched in order to collect all the antlers required. Then the construction of the two great roundhouses—and of the five or six more that there probably were on the rest of the site—would have employed scores of labourers and many skilled carpenters. The massive oak trunks were felled, trimmed away from the site (hardly any axes were found during the excavation) and then, some still weighing 2, or even 5 tonnes, dragged to the earthwork and set up. Rafters and roof beams, wall planks, thatch, interior furnishings and hangings all had to be added. The quantity of flint and stone axes needed must have been very large and there is indeed clear evidence for an upsurge in activity at exactly this time at the Grimes Graves flint mines in Norfolk.

One or two other clues are available about the social status of the people of Durrington Walls. For example, excavations revealed a spindle whorl—the only one so far known from Neolithic Britain. Until this discovery the evidence for Neolithic clothing was in the form of a few antler combs suitable for dressing skins and seemed to point to suits of leather being worn by the majority of the population. Now it is known that woven cloth was almost certainly worn by the henge people—or some of them— and it is difficult to think of a more striking way for one class to distinguish itself than this. An approximate idea of what these clothes may have looked like can be gained from the well known, if slightly later, oak-coffin burials of Denmark, in some of which the bodies of an aristocracy of the succeeding Bronze Age are perfectly preserved fully clothed.

Comparison of the diet of the Durrington people with that of the rural population at large gives further clues. The bones of animals eaten at Durrington Walls presented some peculiar features which could be interpreted as meaning that the meat was brought to the site already slaughtered and cut up, not 'on the hoof'. For example, among the 8,000 or more bones found well preserved in the excavations of 1967 and 1968 there were almost no skulls. Either the skulls were dumped in another part of the site as yet unexplored or carcasses arrived on the site already headless. In either case there is a strong suggestion that butchering was carried out as a specialized activity well away from the two buildings discovered, in other words that there was probably a communal catering establishment—a cookhouse and a refectory perhaps—at Durrington Walls like that tentatively inferred for Skara Brae. This again would fit with the idea that the enclosure was a prehistoric combination of a monastery and a college in which a highly organized community lived, divided into specialized groups and with a staff of cooks, craftsmen and so on. On the whole this seems a simpler and more logical explanation for the curious features of the animal bones than the rather strained ones involving ritual slaughtering which were advanced in the excavation report.

In historical times the members of some monastic orders tilled their own fields and looked after their own flocks and herds. Can we guess whether the inhabitants of Durrington Walls were supplied with meat and other food by the rural population—in the form of taxes or gifts—or whether the community had its own animals and fields? The absence of skulls, commented on above, does perhaps suggest that meat was brought to the site from elsewhere but one could not infer from that alone whose property the beasts originally were. Either solution—that the meat was tribute provided by the peasant population or that it came from animals owned by the henge community—would fit the idea that Durrington Walls might have housed an élite population with retainers and craftsmen.

A clearer picture of the special status of this community is won by looking at what meat they ate and in what quantities. An inhabited Neolithic site not many miles from Durrington Walls, the food refuse of which can be compared with that of the henge site, is the Windmill Hill causewayed camp. There three distinct phases of occupation have been dated by radiocarbon. The first was an occupation before the causewayed camp was built and dated to about the middle of the fourth millennium BC, the second was the primary use of the camp, dated to about 3000 BC, and the third was a late use of the site dated to about 2000 BC. The middens of each phase produced very similar proportions of domestic animal bones, the remains of game being extremely rare (2%–4%); beef was the staple meat, making up between 56% and 67% of the bones, while mutton and pork were much less common, at 12%–24% and 16%–23% respectively. Evidence from quernstones and other domestic articles makes it fairly clear that the people who used Windmill Hill were peasant families camping at the site at intervals to attend fairs or ceremonies or both. It is interesting that over this long period of about 1,500 years they should all have had a very similar diet.

The fact that the site was still being used in late Neolithic times allows us to make a direct comparison with the diet of the Durrington Walls people and we see some striking differences. In the latter case pork was the meat most commonly eaten in the henge: 64% of the identified animals there were pigs. Beef made up 27% while sheep were extremely rare at 2%. These differences again seem to support the belief that the henge was inhabited by a special community.

Pottery and social status

One might expect that the members of a theocratic élite group—or any ruling class—would have special high-quality artefacts, including pottery, made for them by professional craftsmen. Although there is no clear evidence that the users of the chambered tombs had a special pottery the relatively sudden appearance of Grooved ware in middle or late Neolithic times is worth noting, as is its close association with special sites like Durrington Walls, Stonehenge I and Skara Brae.

There are several other features of the ware which might suggest that it was peculiar to one section of society. In the first place, archaeologists have had great difficulty in finding a plausible ancestry for the flat-based Grooved ware among the uniformly round-based bowls of early and middle Neolithic times. Secondly, and again in contrast with other Neolithic wares, no sherd of Grooved ware seems to have been found with a grain impression in it (bearing in mind that the large quantities found in the recent excavations at Skara Brae have not been fully reported on yet). When prehistoric pots were

A spindle whorl discovered at Durrington Walls has been the first evidence that at least some of the henge builders of southern England knew woven cloth. Bone combs suitable for dressing skins (below) had formerly been the only clue to Neolithic clothing in Britain and had pointed only to leather garments. If cloth was worn in the late Neolithic times of Durrington Walls it may have matched fragments found near Stonehenge that date to the early years of the Bronze Age (above) or Bronze Age clothes found in Denmark (right), some of which have been reconstructed (bottom right).

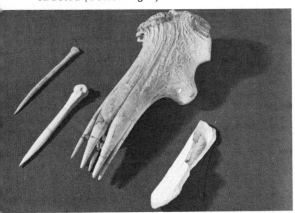

made in a domestic context cereal grains often stuck to the damp clay and left permanent impressions in the vessels on firing. This negative feature of Grooved ware strongly suggests that the pots were made in special workshops by professional potters. Thirdly, the decoration on Grooved ware occasionally includes spirals and concentric rings resembling the 'cup-and-ring' rock carvings of the highland zone and Ireland (and Iberia also). A direct link with the Irish passage graves is to be seen in a 'spiral and lozenge' motif found on a sherd at Skara Brae.

Fourthly, the flat bases of the Grooved ware pots may mean that the vessels stood on flat surfaces—wooden tables and shelves—instead of on an earth floor. The round-based bowls of the early and middle Neolithic people are well suited to standing on soft earth or sand on an uneven hut floor or to being hung from rafters; it seems that an accidental knock would be unlikely to tip such a bowl right over. Flat-based pots to stand on furniture could be a sign of a much higher standard of living.

A correlation between passage graves and stone circles

Since the period of the stone circles and standing stones follows, and partly overlaps with, that of the chambered cairns it seems fair to assume that, if a priesthood were involved with the later monuments, it was descended from similar castes which built the chambered cairns and the long barrows. The two classes of sites also overlap geographically and a derivation of the one from the other is thereby made more plausible. However, stone circles and standing stones are broadly confined to Brittany and the British Isles; the rest of the territory of the megalith builders—Scandinavia, Germany, most of France, Iberia and perhaps Malta—does not have them. And stone circles can occur in large numbers in regions where there are no chambered cairns, as in Aberdeenshire in Scotland. It would help, therefore, if some more direct evidence of cultural continuity between the two kinds of megalithic sites were available.

In the first place it is clear from the Scottish and Irish evidence that passage graves were being used right down to late Neolithic and Chalcolithic times, that is beyond 2500 BC and perhaps in a few cases later than 2000 BC. The number of Beaker period burials found in these and other collective graves is clear evidence of this and a Beaker settlement was found around the New Grange passage grave. The great chambered mound at Knowth may actually have been built at this late time if the radiocarbon date of about 2600 BC for material in the mound is correct. Moreover, the latest dates for the burials in the Quanterness cairn in Orkney make it clear that that building was still being used for interments at around 2500 BC.

In the second place there is a direct connection between a free-standing stone circle and a large, 'advanced' passage grave at New Grange which was built around 3000 BC. Moreover it is possible that both mound and circle were laid out together with 'megalithic' geometry and measuring rods; it is difficult to see how a circle could be added around an already standing, large cairn if it was designed with complex geometry. It is true though that New

Grange is a rarity in this sense; most passage graves lack the free-standing surrounding circle. One other site where standing stones and passage grave are found together is Callanish on Lewis in the Outer Hebrides. Here a stone circle with an attached cross-shaped setting of standing stones surrounds a small passage grave of stalled Orcadian type which looks as if it has been added in later.

The group of Clava cairns at the north-east end of the Great Glen in Inverness-shire includes a number of passage graves with free-standing stone circles around them, one of the best known examples being at Balnuaran of Clava near Culloden moor. Recent work at the Clava cairn at Raigmore has provided the first radiocarbon dates for this class of monument, the chronology of which has hitherto been a matter of dispute. The dates fall towards the end of the fourth millennium BC and imply that the cairn was contemporary with New Grange. Moreover, the discovery that New Grange was orientated in a very skilful manner towards the midwinter sunrise—and in a way that surely confirms that the domed chamber into which the sun's rays shone was the heart of a temple—matches in a quite startling way the similar orientation of the passages of two of the cairns at Balnuaran of Clava.

These resemblances leave little room for doubt that the Clava cairns, in their primary passage grave form, were built as an outpost of the Boyne passage graves of Ireland and that some of the stone circles—probably most of those in north-east Scotland—are derived from this intrusive group. Some at least of the circle builders—with all their inherited or acquired expertise in religion, geometry and astronomy and living as they seem to have done as separate castes—were perhaps descended directly from the passage grave builders of Ireland.

The origins of the megalith builders

There can be little doubt that the standing stones were a regional development in north-west Europe, a remarkable local device for accurate astronomical observation. But the question remains about these as well as about the Maltese temples and the Iberian, Breton, Irish, British and Scandinavian passage graves and other collective tombs: were the *people* who designed and organized them also indigenous, or were they in each case immigrants who brought professional practices with them? Did they in this case hybridize genetically and culturally with the leaders of the local Neolithic population to produce characteristically local and vital versions of the 'megalithic culture'?

Evidence is steadily accumulating, first, that the builders of the standing stones and stone circles of Britain and Brittany were probably organized in castes or orders of professionals. Thanks to the work of Thom their expertise in late Neolithic times can be proved and can now be matched with the rest of the archaeological evidence without undue strain. There is also plenty of evidence that passage graves, and other monumental collective 'tombs', were being used and even built in late Neolithic times.

There are fewer and fewer signs of a gap in the evolution of the 'megalith builders' from early to late Neolithic times.

Indeed as more and more radiocarbon dates become available this picture of continuity becomes ever clearer. For example, the first phase of occupation at Skara Brae in Orkney—diagnosed here as a specialist community perhaps of priests or wise men—is now known to have taken place at about 3100 BC, at almost the same time that New Grange was built. The Stenness stone circle nearby was also built at about 3000 BC and, having yielded Grooved ware, is likely to be linked with the first occupants of the village. Burials in the Quanterness chambered cairn—an Orkney version of the passage grave—took place at about the same time. Who can say that these people, thus interred in splendour, were not members of the ruling theocracy of the time and who will deny now that the final burials in Quanterness cairn, dated to exactly the same time as the occupation of the main village of Skara Brae at around 2500 BC, could not have been later members of the same caste?

The conclusion seems inescapable that the builders of passage graves and stone circles were members of professional priesthoods whose traditions were continuous from early to late Neolithic times and may have lasted even longer. These ruling groups possibly included a lay aristocracy. In this view the first great phase of megalith building—from Iberia to Britain and Scandinavia—represents the migrations of members of a new dominant class, composed of or at least guided by professional priests and wise men, who settled successfully among the recently established Neolithic farming populations of Atlantic Europe. By mixing and hybridizing they formed the top level of a variety of local stratified societies, dominated by the priesthood, and with a strong common genetic and cultural element. The rite of collective burial, inside monumental structures which possibly also served as focal points for the religions and as symbols of authority, would in this case be the way in which the élite group would emphasize its dominance and keep apart in death as in life.

The people collectively buried in the chambered long cairns and unchambered long barrows of England and Scotland are racially almost indistinguishable—a circumstance which fits well with the idea that they were all members of a genetically related and stable caste. Earlier commentators thought that the same kind of skulls had been found in the Iberian chambered tombs and there is other genetic evidence—from blood groups, hair colour and other anatomical features—for the survival in parts of western Britain and Ireland of people descended from a west Mediterranean stock. Language too may tell a similar story; C. D. Darlington showed in 1954, for instance, how the distribution of people who pronounce 'th' as 't' is now concentrated in only two isolated pockets in Atlantic Europe—in Portugal and south-west Ireland—perhaps a relic of the population of megalithic times.

Meanwhile, working from purely archaeological data, what conclusions can be reached? If the passage graves can be plausibly interpreted as the temple-tombs of a relatively sophisticated professional priesthood, or religious élite of some kind, which practised collective burial, and the long barrows and cairns as the monuments of a different but related branch which emerged and flourished specifically in northern Europe and Britain, there can be little doubt that this priesthood began the major part of its career in Iberia where the passage graves almost certainly originated. What is known of the ethnic features of the associated skulls (and other related modern anatomical data) supports this view; the Iberian and northern skulls are sometimes described as a Eurafrican branch of the Mediterranean race and might support the idea that the caste emerged in Iberia by means of the hybridization there of more than one stock. It is indeed tempting to link the appearance of a characteristically European Atlantic form of religious monument with the appearance of a characteristically Atlantic European taxon of people associated with it and to see the resulting stable religious caste as spreading steadily northwards, taking institutions, religion and rules of recruitment and intermarriage with them.

The influence of Portugal

Further striking evidence of the movement northwards from Iberia of members of a professional caste in middle and late Neolithic times is available. In reviewing developments among the megalith-building cultures of north-west Europe in late Neolithic times several points about the origins of the stone-circle builders were left unanswered, in particular the origin of the esoteric skills now visible in the circles and standing stone sites and that of the Grooved ware so closely associated with Skara Brae and the ceremonial centres of southern England. It seems reasonable to assume that one or more of the theocratic groups practising communal burial, which have been inferred for the Neolithic period, developed its geometrical and astronomical knowledge, and skills in surveying and measuring, to a high degree and produced a new religion based on temple-observatories built with standing stones. On the basis of the knowledge available at present these important developments seem most likely to have started among the passage grave builders of the Boyne valley of Ireland and culminated on the chalk lands of southern England. The reasons for thinking this include the existence of a stone circle round New Grange which ought to be contemporary with the passage grave, the astronomical and geometrical properties of that monument, the link between Irish passage grave art and Grooved ware seen in the 'spirals-and-lozenges' and in other motifs and, finally and most important, the general proposition maintained here that the passage grave builders brought the basis of such advanced knowledge with them from Iberia.

It might be necessary to stress again at this point that to believe in the Iberian origins of the skills seen in the stone circles need not lessen the degree of ingenuity and inventiveness of the local theocratic groups of eastern Ireland—or wherever it was—which evolved what one supposes was a new sky-orientated religion with a basis in exact astronomical observation. A

Darwinian interpretation of these events would make us suppose that the Breton, Irish and British passage grave builders themselves were the results of several successive stages of travel, hybridization and social mixing by élite groups (starting in Iberia) and that the stone circle cults grew up in north-west Atlantic Europe out of one of these early Neolithic religious groups. The material equipment, the use of megalithic standing stones as well as the details of religious beliefs and rituals were probably locally devised just as most of the priests could have been local people, descended over many generations from the original hybrid innovators. However, the institution of the professional priestly caste itself, as well as its original members in each area and the basis of its inherited specialized knowledge and wisdom would have been of foreign origin.

The Grooved ware people seem to have been one of the major theocratic groups in late Neolithic Britain. And at Skara Brae—the most important northern outpost of this class of people—was found a set of curious stone implements closely matched by objects in the Chalcolithic rock-cut tombs of the Tagus estuary area in Portugal. The first assessment of the Skara Brae pottery (now called Grooved ware) by V. G. Childe also drew attention to Portuguese Copper Age parallels and there do seem to be fairly clear connections between the ornament of Grooved ware and some designs found on decorated stones in Irish passage graves. Were it not for the fact that very little proper Grooved ware has so far been found in Ireland one would be tempted to suggest that the ceremonial centres in southern England were built for and inhabited by a rejuvenated branch of the theocratic group of the Boyne valley.

Under the influence of the prevailing anti-diffusionist climate in archaeological thought, which makes one choose a local origin for everything unless there is very strong evidence for the contrary, it can be suggested that Grooved ware was a pottery developed in Wessex specially for the theocratic élite groups who lived in the ceremonial centres there and that its shape and decoration reflected the partial Irish origin of these people as well as their special status.

However, many of the Chalcolithic Tagus tombs contained very characteristic, possibly imported pots—a dark brown ware ornamented profusely with channelled decoration, which has strong links with the Aegean in the Early Bronze Age and with Anatolia. These vessels, known as *copos* to Portuguese archaeologists, are often hemispherical but many have a flat base. At Vila Nova de São Pedro they were largely found in a layer associated with the occupation before the building of the citadel with bastioned walls, so there they may date to around the beginning of the third millennium BC. The decoration of some of these pots is surprisingly like that of some British Grooved ware pots as is the shape of the vessels themselves.

If Grooved ware were indeed a British version of the Portuguese *copos* the late Neolithic connections between the two areas would be reinforced and the sum total of the evidence for it, as well as its variety, would be quite impressive—it ranges from units of measurement, through rock carvings and stone implements to pottery and plaques—and it would be hard to deny that influence from Chalcolithic Portugal played an important part in the genesis of the Grooved ware culture. Perhaps Portugal also played a prominent role in the creation of the late Neolithic astronomy-based religion with its standing stone observatories, despite its strong roots in the passage grave period.

Until recently the dating of the Portuguese channelled ware was apparently a little too early to suit this hypothesis when compared with that of British Grooved ware. In Portugal it seems to have been used at Vila Nova de São Pedro at around 3000 BC or even a little earlier. Until 1975 the earliest unequivocal date for British Grooved ware was for pieces found in the primary silts of the ditch at Stonehenge, dated to about the 29th century BC. But now we know that the primary occupation of Skara Brae was before 3000 BC and that Grooved ware was used in this first occupation of the village. The same pottery came from an early context in the Stenness stone circle, also in Orkney, again dated by Carbon 14 to about 3000 BC. The time gap between the suggested Portuguese prototype and British Grooved ware seems to have disappeared.

Of great significance too is the fact that the exceptionally finely built passage grave at Quanterness in Orkney has yielded Grooved ware with its numerous burials—the first such megalithic tomb to have done so—and that the earliest of these interments so far dated were put in at the end of the fourth millennium BC at the time the first village at Skara Brae was built, when New Grange was constructed and not long before the building of the stone circle at Stenness, Orkney (where Grooved ware was also found). The impact of the appearance of people using Grooved ware is clearly seen—in the construction of architecturally sophsticated temple-tombs (some perhaps with astronomical orientations incorporated in them), in the building of special stone residences, and in some early stone circles which could have been astronomical observatories also. Such an outburst of varied activity, which continued into late Neolithic times in some remarkable developments in southern England, shows clearly that the Grooved ware people were a special class and perhaps reinforces the suggestion that at least some part of their origin lay in Portugal.

Ships and sea routes

In the light of the abundant archaeological evidence for contact between the different populations along the Atlantic coasts of Europe between 4500 and 2500 BC it is worth looking briefly at the technical problems of sea travel that might have been involved. Models and carvings provide some clues. For example, a clay model of a sailing boat was found in a fifth or fourth millennium BC grave at Eridu in Mesopotamia, and might represent a skin-covered vessel. Boats with high prows and sterns are seen in the pictograms of the succeeding period in Mesopotamia and by the mid-third millennium BC quite elaborate rowing and sailing vessels are shown in bas-reliefs at Saqqara in Egypt.

A Maltese temple bears carving of boats, as do two megalithic sites in Brittany, including Mané Lud (above). Stones of the Early Bronze Age in Denmark (left) carry the earliest representations of more northerly vessels. All appear to show what would have been a likely sort of craft in the circumstances of the time — a skin-covered canoe with a crew of paddlers and perhaps with sails as well.

Of boats to sail the tidal seas of northern Europe, however, we have little evidence, apart from dug-out canoes, before the Bronze Age rock carvings of Scandinavia. Most of these carvings—which are broadly dated to the second millennium BC—are likely to be representations of large, skin-covered canoes paddled by sizeable crews. However, one vessel of the same period, on a bronze sword blade from Rørby in Denmark, has been likened to a Mediterranean war galley, with the characteristic eye on the bow, a ram clearly depicted under this and the 30 starboard rowers shown. Whoever designed the Bronze Age sword had very probably seen such a warship. Whether that means that it had been rowed up to the Baltic is another matter, though that might just be possible when one considers that Carthaginian galleys seem to have reached Brittany in the fifth century BC.

For the preceding, Neolithic period the evidence is scanty. Two Breton megaliths, Petit Mont and Mané Lud, have what may be ship carvings on them; the former seems to show a vessel with a cabin and closely resembles not only some of the Scandinavian carvings but also ship carvings in the Tarxien temple in Malta. The megalith builders probably had to travel in large, skin-covered boats with a crew of paddlers and perhaps with sails as well.

There is a fine natural harbour at Cadiz just outside the Straits of Gibraltar and similar good natural harbours in which to anchor for the night are to be found every 60 or 80 kilometres to Oporto, about half-way up the west coast of Iberia. Thereafter the coast to Finistère (the north-west 'corner' of Iberia) has creeks and inlets about every 15 kilometres so that nightly stops would have been no problem. However, a half knot current runs steadily southwards along the whole of this coast and the prevailing wind blows in the same direction. Navigation of the north coast of Spain is fairly straightforward but there can be dangerous swells, caused by conflicting currents, where France and Spain meet. Up to Brittany the tides are moderate but in the Channel the rise and fall of the sea can be much greater than further south and the currents are constantly changing. Such rough sea conditions are to be found in many places round the British Isles and, everything considered, it is difficult to believe that the various groups of passage grave and other megalith builders could have been in frequent contact. Early voyages in paddled skin boats or small sailing ships were therefore very probably intermittent and would have taken a long time. However, rare and difficult though they might have been, voyages of small numbers of important people would conform with the wide distribution of the passage graves around the northern seas. And our theocratic groups may have had the services of skilled local seamen familiar with the local tides and currents.

Chapter XII   The Foundations of Western Europe

Thus far I have tried in this book to show that an evolutionary explanation for the development and spread of the Atlantic European megaliths will fit the archaeological evidence at least as well as, and I think better than, non-diffusionist theories of random independent development. This evolutionary view is that which involves a modern form of diffusionism—the movement, and genetic and cultural mingling, of small numbers of specialized and skilled people, but without a mass of what one might call cultural luggage and not in the form of organized colonising expeditions from an urban civilization.

Not the least of the advantages, it seems to me, of this Darwinian approach to prehistoric cultural evolution is that it specifies what is likely to have happened in terms familiar to students of living societies. Instead of undefined cultural processes or influences, or open-ended assumptions about local inventiveness or capacities for exchanging ideas, we have a picture of the evolution of a specific institution—professional priesthood in this case—and of the physical movement of some of its members to new territories together with their special knowledge and skills. These energetic newcomers and their hybrid descendants would create out of local resources and imported ideas a vigorous new theocratic culture which, in favourable circumstances, would develop from small beginnings to something quite elaborate.

Neither does this kind of interpretation have to ignore or play down archaeological facts, such as the uniformity of passage graves over a wide area, the even wider distribution of collective burial or the fact that the 'megalithic' cultures of Iberia were richer and more numerous than those to the north.

I have assumed that something dramatic happened to Neolithic society in Iberia in the early or mid-fifth millennium BC and resulted in the appearance of a dynamic, characteristically Atlantic European professional priesthood with its own body of ritual and knowledge and its typical temple-tombs in which the members of the orders were interred over many generations. If Darlington's hypothesis about the causes of most dramatic cultural changes is approximately correct, we might expect the beginnings of these developments to be due to the genetic and cultural mixing of two or more different ethnic groups of talented people and the creation in this way of a vigorous hybrid people and culture and a complex stratified society. Are there any clues to the nature of the various parts of this mixture? Could it be that the professional priesthood itself did not arise in Iberia but was brought there from elsewhere, perhaps from the proto-urban societies of the Near East?

In many ways it might be better to end this book without pursuing this problem since theories involving the diffusion of advanced culture out of the Near East or, more usually, Egypt have a long history of bias and extremism. The easy solution would be to forget all that and let the hypothesis proposed here rest on the Atlantic European evidence alone. Its acceptance would probably thereby be made easier since the spectre of Perry's 'children of the Sun' carrying advanced culture from Egypt all over the world would not be raised.

In spite of all this there is a clear duty to investigate the possibility that our supposed megalithic priesthood did ultimately originate further east than Iberia, not least because one of the fundamental tenets of the modern anti-diffusionist doctrines is that the European megaliths are too old to have been affected by the world's first urban civilization in Mesopotamia.

The megalithic measuring system

The megalithic measuring system provides one clue to the origin of the institution of priesthood itself and of its more esoteric knowledge. A system of exact measurement based on a unit of just over $32\frac{1}{2}$ inches (0·829 metres) and known as the megalithic yard was discovered quite independently to have been used in the late Neolithic standing stone sites of Britain as well as in those of Brittany. This unit could have been used in several places in the ancient world and certainly survived into modern times in places as diverse as north-west India, Iberia and the Austrian Tyrol.

For example, the traditional unit of length known as the *gaz* was in use as late as the nineteenth century in north-west India when it was standardized at exactly 33 inches (0·838 metres) by the British government. In the 1930s excavations at Mohenjo-daro, one of the oldest city mounds in India and part of the Bronze Age Indus civilization, radiocarbon dates for which show that it must have been contemporary with Early Dynastic Sumeria and Old Kingdom Egypt, revealed a small piece of shell, part of a longer piece and with nine exactly equal divisions still remaining which had been cut into it with a fine saw. Five of these small divisions evidently made up a larger unit the boundaries of which were marked with a dot on the line. A. E. Berriman has pointed out that 25 of the major divisions, now called 'Indus inches', totalled exactly 33 inches, the same length as the traditional *gaz*. It is difficult not to believe that the metrology of these Bronze Age cities was handed down intact over 45 centuries.

Berriman also worked out the length of some small Sumerian length units from scales cut into stone statues of Governor Gudea of Lagash in

Mesopotamia who lived in about 2200 BC. These units, which he thought were probably the *shusi* mentioned in the cuneiform texts, were on average exactly half the 'Indus inch'. Thus there were 50 Sumerian *shusi* in the traditional Indian *gaz*. Stone weights found at Mohenjo-daro also seem to be related to the Mesopotamian system. Both the *shusi* and the units of weight were perpetuated in Greek, Roman and Saxon metrology.

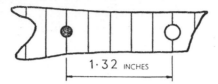

1·32 INCHES

It is the distance between the circle and the dot on a fragment of shell found in the Indus Valley that has been termed the Indus inch.

A traditional short yard of just over 33 inches, known as the *vara*, was in use in Iberia until recently and was evidently taken to Mexico and Peru by the Spanish conquerors. And Iberia was probably the place of origin of the passage graves and one might hazard a guess that the *vara* is at least as old as those Neolithic and Chalcolithic monuments. Further hints of the use of this ancient system are to be found in the measuring rods used from time immemorial by mine overseers in the Austrian Tyrol which are exactly 33 inches long. Mining has been carried out in the Tyrol since the Early Bronze Age at least.

It is now known that an almost exactly similar 'short yard' of just over $32\frac{1}{2}$ inches was in use in Britain and Brittany in the latter part of the third millennium BC, and, in the light of this other evidence just reviewed, it would be difficult to maintain any more that the measuring system used by the circle builders was an isolated north-west European phenomenon. It is especially significant that New Grange is now proved to be an advanced cruciform passage grave dating to about 3000 BC, in the design of which there is clear evidence of both the astronomical and the measuring and geometrical skills which appear widely in the stone circles of the late Neolithic and Early Bronze Age. The monument is of course surrounded by the remains of a stone circle. Although the rest of the Atlantic European passage graves have yet to be systematically searched for such attributes, New Grange gives a very strong hint that the advanced intellectual culture of the stone circle builders, which reached its zenith at Stonehenge, had its roots in the passage graves—which themselves have their roots in Iberia, where the measuring rod survived into modern times. Is it possible that the institution of priesthood itself came from Mesopotamia?

The first cities

The chronology worked out for the development of the oldest known urban society—that of southern Mesopotamia—shows that true cities did not appear until about the middle of the fourth millennium BC, some 1,000 years later than the earliest megaliths. This is the foundation of the new anti-diffusionist interpretation of the development of the megalith builders of prehistoric Europe. If the European megaliths, and even the Maltese temples, are older than the oldest towns then it is difficult to see how urban societies could have played any significant part in the great social processes which were under way in Atlantic Europe between 4500 and 2500 BC.

An urban society may be defined as one in which a substantial proportion of the total population of a given area lives in one or more towns and, more important, is one whose members are mainly engaged full time in non-agricultural pursuits like being merchants, shop-keepers, traders, coppersmiths, tailors, soldiers, priests, engineers, craftsmen, kings, generals and so on.

A town provides a vastly greater range of activities for individuals to follow than could ever have been available in a rural peasant society but, to make such a society possible, the farming population has to be persuaded or forced to grow far more food than it needs for itself in order to feed the townspeople and allow them to practise and improve their specialized skills for the whole time. Once established as going concerns the towns attract people from the countryside who are ambitious or whose temperaments make them unsuited to a farming life, or simply because younger sons cannot usually inherit the father's land. In the city numerous new classes emerge, usually defined by their occupation or trade, as many different individuals and groups adapt to the new opportunities presented. Originating in widespread social mixing and hybridization—which produces even more varieties of people and combinations of talents—these classes then tend to solidify in primitive cities and to erect barriers around themselves by devising rules against outbreeding for their members. Hereditary professions and trades are very common in pre-industrial cities.

In Palaeolithic and Neolithic times the process of social and genetic evolution is one of the steady separation of the hunting and farming communities which become geographically isolated and genetically, culturally and linguistically diverse. With the rise of the earliest towns the process starts to be reversed and a high degree of mixing, interbreeding and the re-arrangement of social groups takes place in the new, crowded environment to form complex, stratified societies having a great variety of skills and talents. Once urbanization had advanced to the point of being an efficient way of life (based of course on efficient agriculture), the tendency would be for it to spread outwards from its primary centres through the migration of the skilled specialists who were its products. Unlike the peasants, who have to stay with their land come what may, the more skilled city people usually move to where their talents are best employed.

The emergence of urban man is thus a crucially important event in human history; after the time that this began on a large scale it cannot be denied that the effects of city life, of city needs and of city people must have reached steadily further and further out among the Neolithic hinterlands around the primary centres of urbanization. In Europe the process reached its first culmination in the conquests of Imperial Rome and the full scale urbanization of western European society.

193

The question is, when were the effects of the development of the earliest town first felt in Europe. Taking, with Renfrew, an essentially Lamarckian view, there is no difficulty in supposing that technically and intellectually advanced cultures could have emerged anywhere in Europe simply because of local factors. In this case the rise of the Near Eastern cities would probably have been irrelevant to the problem of the European megaliths. If, on the other hand, a Darwinian view is taken, major, non-utilitarian technological changes (of the kind that involve specialized skills beyond those required for a farming existence), which are found over a wide area, are quite likely to have come about because of the arrival of a few influential people possessing those skills. This is not to say, of course, that such innovations will not occasionally appear in isolation—the Danish megalithic *dysser* may be a case in point—but only that if they are successful and widespread they may well mark the appearance of some new and energetic men directly or indirectly of urban origin.

It must be clear that, if the latter interpretation is about right, then there must have been specialized, proto-urban or urban stratified societies in existence before the earliest megaliths appeared and that this is a crucial test for the theories propounded in this book. Although to the authors of recent publications on the subject it has seemed certain that the rise of the Mesopotamian cities occurred much later than the spread of collective burial and megalithic building into Neolithic Atlantic Europe, the alternative view must maintain that either there is a fallacy in the evidence on which this view is based or that the conclusions themselves are wrong. If the tree-ring calibration of radiocarbon dates is about right one interpretation of the spread of collective burial, and of the skills that evidently went with it, must predict that more advanced societies were in existence and flourishing somewhere by 5000 BC or soon after—early enough to allow time for their effects to spread westwards in the way described. Is this possible?

Evidence for the dating of the earliest urban societies—accepted as solid and dependable by the anti-diffusionist school—is highly speculative. The evidence was first set out in detail, and its implications for European prehistory explained, by V. G. Childe in 1934, and was largely based on Sir Leonard Woolley's excavations at the city of Ur. These culminated, as far as dating is concerned, in his discovery in 1924 of an inscription referring to A-anni-padda, the founder of the First Dynasty at Ur and who probably lived near the beginning of the third millennium BC. Previously there had been no reliable historical evidence for the period before the mid-third millennium BC.

The historical dates were based partly on the Babylonian king lists with their reign lengths and partly on archaeological links between Sumer and Egypt where the earliest historical period has its own absolute chronology. These are supported by a few radiocarbon dates for bones of identified people of Ur of the late Early Dynastic period, which is usually thought to have ended in about the 24th century BC. When the tree-ring correction factor is applied these dates become about the same as the historical dates and it can now be assumed with new confidence that the Early Dynastic period did begin soon after 3000 BC.

Childe's reconstruction of the earlier development of the world's oldest cities had to be done on the basis of Woolley's deep soundings at Ur which, though limited in extent, showed that the Early Dynastic period had very much older, prehistoric roots. But in 1946–49 the Iraqi government sponsored excavations which made some exciting new discoveries at Eridu, another ancient city mound in the delta in southern Mesopotamia.

At Eridu, under a corner of the great Third Dynasty ziggurat were found the remains of no less than 17 former temples, one on top of the ruins of another. The range of archaeological material in the successively lower levels of use of the site extended in date right back to include pottery in the style of early Neolithic ware from northern Mesopotamia. The drainage and colonization of the swampy delta had obviously taken place much earlier in Neolithic times than had been supposed, and the temple-dominated way of life had its origins far back in time, at the very dawn of civilized life.

The chronology of these remarkable developments is obscure. Before the First Dynasty dates are mainly guesses, extrapolations back from the historical dates and based on estimates of how long each reconstructed temple might have lasted before being replaced. And it had become an article of unquestioned faith that true city life began at about 3500 BC.

But there is now a radiocarbon date of about 4900 or 5000 BC for some reeds taken from the very base of the temple complex, which rested on virgin soil, at Uruk, another delta town. The reeds should mark the foundation of the temple at that site. Another radiocarbon date of well before 5000 BC, from Tell Uqair, may also be linked with the same period, and a series of dates from Tepe Gawra show that a northern version of a contemporary culture was flourishing in the sixth millennium BC.

The crucial point is that there is very clear evidence for the development of a powerful professional priesthood, and therefore of the beginnings of an efficient, stratified proto-urban society, in southern Mesopotamia at a very early date—probably before 5000 BC. At Eridu, as the archaeology suggests, the process may have begun even earlier. It is difficult to overestimate the potential importance of this discovery; even if true towns with large populations including many trades and professions were not in existence until well on in the fifth millennium BC, or even not until the fourth, the social evolution which led up to them must have begun much earlier and well before the rise of the European megalith-builders. It does not seem possible any more to deny on chronological grounds that the emerging professional priesthoods in Mesopotamia could have had profound direct or indirect effects on the organization of Neolithic societies in the western Mediterranean and Atlantic Europe by the middle of the fifth millennium BC.

A religious revolution?

That there was a religious impulse behind the appearance of collective burial in the Mediterranean and in Atlantic Europe is most clearly seen in Malta where true temples were evolved soon after the arrival or appearance of the rite of collective burial on the island. But nearly everywhere in Atlantic Europe the appearance of the rite is followed by the development of monumental drystone tombs and then by the slow but steady improvement in their design in characteristically local ways. The passage graves are a good example and these—especially the larger, more sophisticated one—could easily have been temples as well as tombs. Their elaborate architecture, the presence of stone basins and carvings in some in Iberia and Ireland, as well as the striking astronomical orientation of New Grange, all strongly suggest that they were built at the behest of a priestly class.

These long-held feelings that the European megaliths were the creation of religious groups of some kind can now be combined well with the new evidence for the very early development of temples and priesthoods in the rise of the first urban civilizations in the Near East to suggest a general explanation, or hypothesis, to account for the megalith builders and their origins. Drawing a broad analogy with the primary spread of agriculture and the Neolithic way of life it is possible to suppose that there was a very important, and possibly long-lasting stage between the first expansion of the agriculturalists and the first spread of true urban life. In this intermediate stage might have occurred the appearance and expansion of the professional priesthoods of southern Mesopotamia in the fifth millennium BC in a sort of religious revolution.

Temple complexes appear in southern Mesopotamia probably as soon as the colonization of that region was under way, and certainly long before proper urban societies had developed at Uruk, Eridu and other sites. The appearance of efficient Neolithic farmers some millennia earlier in the same area evidently set in motion a slow but steady expansion of the farming population which eventually influenced the remotest regions. In the same way the appearance of efficient professional priesthoods—their members selected for their skill in dominating the peasant population intellectually and emotionally and in extracting tribute and wealth from them—might similarly have set in motion the steady outward spread of people wanting to practise this new and comparatively civilized way of life. The whole phenomenon of the European collective tombs could well be explicable in terms of the movement of such professional theocrats, their hybridization with and recruitment of local people of a similar kind, the appearance of local sects and imitations, the great success of some groups and comparative failure of others and so on. As always in such circumstances the adoption and adaptation of local customs and beliefs must have been an important key to success—hence the variety in the material cultures found in the collective tombs or the tendency to prefer cremation in some areas. Nevertheless, the underlying unity seems to be there and the passage graves provide hard archaeological evidence for the importance of Iberia in developing a successful European brand of Neolithic theocracy out of the Mediterranean forms.

It has now been shown that temple complexes, presumably with professional priesthoods, must have developed in southern Mesopotamia in the 5th millennium BC long before the rise of true urban society. Their sophistication is represented today only by the crumbling ziggurat and outlying building foundations at such later sites as Agar Kuf (above). The megalith builders were making themselves apparent at the same time and it is no longer possible to say that the 5th millennium appearance of such specialist groups among Neolithic farming communities in Atlantic Europe was entirely without contemporary example. Long-held feelings have been strengthened that the megalith builders too were professional theocrats.

The avenue at Avebury, part of one of the megalith builders' biggest ceremonial centres.

The foundations of western Europe

It is usually thought that the distinctiveness of the peoples, the traditions and the institutions of western Europe is largely due to their common Roman heritage, on the fact that the Roman Empire included the whole of the area west of the Rhine and the Danube (except Ireland and Scotland) for up to five centuries. During this time there was imposed on what had previously been a heterogeneous collection of barbarian tribes an ordered urban civilization which was essentially the same from Hadrian's Wall to Palestine.

However, the process of transforming primitive Neolithic peasant communities into more advanced, stratified societies with skilled leaders and wise men as well as other specialists, may have begun very much earlier. If our hypothesis of a Religious Revolution is approximately correct it began with the progressively wider establishment of professional priesthoods in early Neolithic times, from about 4500 BC, and the importation by these of specialized knowledge and skills originating where the institution of professional priesthood itself presumably originated, in proto-urban southern Mesopotamia perhaps as early as 5000 BC. The megalithic cairns and other collective tombs should be the temples and graves of these priesthoods—their variety reflecting the adaption of the castes to local conditions—and the descendants of these groups should have begun the remarkable north-west European developments in astronomy and other civilized skills in the third millennium BC. It must have been these people who founded the permanent religious and learned orders which lasted thousands of years and which gave such a distinctive character to pre-Roman Europe and to the culture of the surviving un-Romanized parts—Celtic Ireland and Scotland.

It is possible that sea voyages, if infrequent, kept these theocratic groups in touch with each other during the Neolithic period—especially the passage grave builders, who seem to have been a very special group—and that this was why some large Iberian passage graves were used for rites involving stone basins in the same way as some on the river Boyne. However, a fresh northward movement of skilled, semi-urban people from Portugal—who seem to have benefited shortly before from renewed contacts with the Aegean and the Near East—evidently occurred early in the third millennium BC. These presumably mixed with the established leaders in Ireland and Britain and then created a remarkable energetic and gifted theocratic group based on southern England. The circular megalithic temples and observatories of this new theocracy and its offshoots became widespread over Britain, presumably demonstrating that a new religion or cult—perhaps based on the sun and the moon and requiring accurate observatories—succeeded all over Brittany and the British Isles. Thus perhaps were the basic elements of a civilized society introduced by the megalith builders into the rural, tribal environment of Neolithic Atlantic Europe.

Further reading

Ashbee, Paul, *The earthen long barrow in Britain* (London, 1970).

Atkinson, R. J. C., *Stonehenge* (Harmondsworth, 1960).

Baker, John R., *Race* (Oxford, 1974).

Banbury, Philip, *Man and the sea; from the Ice Age to the Norman Conquest* (London, 1975).

Cary, M. and Warmington, E. H., *The ancient explorers* (Revised edition: Harmondsworth, 1963).

Childe, V. G., *Skara Brae: a Pictish village in Orkney* (London, 1931).

—— *New light on the most ancient east* (London, 1934).

—— *Man makes himself* (London, 1936).

Clarke, D. V., *The Neolithic village at Skara Brae, Orkney: 1972–73 excavations: an interim report* (Edinburgh, 1976).

Daniel, G. E., *The prehistoric chamber tombs of England and Wales* (Cambridge, 1950).

—— *The first civilisations: the archaeology of their origins* (London, 1968).

Darlington, C. D., *The evolution of man and society* (Oxford, 1968).

Ehrich, Robert W. (Ed.), *Chronologies in Old World archaeology* (Chicago, 1965).

Evans, J. D., *Malta* (London, 1959).

Giot, P. R., *Brittany* (London, 1960).

Hadingham, Evan, *Circles and standing stones* (London, 1975).

Hawkins, G. S., *Stonehenge decoded* (London, 1965).

Henshall, Audrey, *The chambered tombs of Scotland* (Two volumes: Edinburgh, 1963 and 1972).

MacKie, Euan W., *Science and society in prehistoric Britain* (London, 1977).

O'Riordain, Sean P. and Daniel, Glyn, *New Grange* (London, 1964).

Piggott, S., *Neolithic cultures of the British Isles* (Cambridge, 1954).

Piggott, S., McBurney, C. and Daniel, G. E. (Eds.), *France before the Romans* (London, 1974).

Renfrew, Colin, *Before civlisation* (London, 1973).

—— (Ed.), *British prehistory: a new outline* (London, 1974).

Roux, Georges, *Ancient Iraq* (Harmondsworth, 1966).

Savory, H. N., *Spain and Portugal* (London, 1968).

Stone, J. F. S., *Wessex before the Celts* (London, 1958).

Thom, Alexander, *Megalithic sites in Britain* (Oxford, 1967).

Trump, D. H., *Malta: an archaeological guide* (London, 1972).

Wainwright, G. J., 'Religion and settlement in Wessex 3000–1700 bc' in P. J. Fowler (Ed.), *Recent work in rural archaeology* (Bradford on Avon, 1974).

List of illustrations

23 (bottom) Pottery, flints and bone points of the Rinyo-Clacton culture. From Woodhenge, Wiltshire, England. Salisbury and South Wiltshire Museum. Photo: Stanley Thomas.

29 (top) Mġarr, Malta. Central court of the second temple. Photo: Euan MacKie.

29 (bottom) Haġar Qim, Malta. General view of the temples. Photo by courtesy of the Malta Government Tourist Office.

31 (top) Tarxien, Malta. General view of the first and second temples. Photo: Robert Estall.

31 (bottom) Tarxien, Malta. Detail of stone carving in the temples. Photo: Robert Estall.

31 (bottom right) Mnajdra, Malta. Temple doorway. Photo: Robert Estall.

39 (top) Cardial ware pot. From the Cova de l'Or, Alicante, Spain. Photo: Servicio de Investigacion Prehistorica, Valencia.

39 (bottom left) Cardial ware pot. From the Cova de l'Or, Alicante, Spain. Photo: Servicio de Investigacion Prehistorica, Valencia.

39 (bottom right) Alapraia 1, Estremadura, Portugal. General view of the rock-cut tomb. Photo reproduced by permission of R. J. Harrison.

43 Dolmen de Soto, Huelva, Spain. Interior of the chambered tomb. Photo by courtesy of the Spanish National Tourist Office.

47 (top) Vila Nova de São Pedro, Ribatejo, Portugal. Wall of the citadel of the Chalcolithic castro. Photo: H. N. Savory.

47 (bottom) Almizaraque, Almeria, Spain. Forecourt of a tomb in the cemetery of the Chalcolithic settlement. Photo reproduced by permission of R. J. Harrison.

53 (top) Dolmen de l'Ile aux Moines, Morbihan, France. Photo by courtesy of the French Government Tourist Office.

53 (bottom) La Roché aux Fées, Ille-et-Vilaine, France. Photo by courtesy of the French Government Tourist Office.

55 (top) Table des Marchands, Morbihan, France. Entrance to the passage grave and view of the Grand Menhir Brisé. Photo: Robert Estall.

55 (bottom) Table des Marchands, Morbihan, France. Interior of the passage grave. Photo by courtesy of the French Government Tourist Office.

56 Table des Marchands, Morbihan, France. Decorated stone in the cham-

ber of the passage grave. Photo by courtesy of the French Government Tourist Office.

59 (top) Table des Marchands, Morbihan, France. Carving of a hafted axe. Photo: Robert Estall.

59 (bottom) Dolmen de Mané Rutual, Morbihan, France. Serpentiform carving. Photo: Robert Estall.

65 (top) Knowth, Co. Meath, Ireland. Decorated kerbstone of the eastern passage grave. Photo: George Eogan.

65 (centre) Knowth, Co. Meath, Ireland. Decorated kerbstone of the eastern passage grave. Photo: George Eogan.

65 (bottom) Knowth, Co. Meath, Ireland. Decorated kerbstone of the western passage grave. Photo: George Eogan.

73 (top) New Grange, Co. Meath, Ireland. General view of the passage grave. Photo by courtesy of M. J. O'Kelly.

73 (bottom) Carrowmore, Co. Sligo, Ireland. Photo: Mansell Collection.

77 (top) West Kennett, Wiltshire, England. Air view of the chambered long barrow. Photo: Aerofilms Ltd.

77 (centre) West Kennet, Wiltshire, England. Interior of the gallery and entrance to a side-chamber. British Crown copyright; reproduced by permission of Her Britannic Majesty's Stationery Office.

77 (bottom) West Kennett, Wiltshire, England. Facade of the chambered long barrow. Photo: Janet Bord.

78 (top) Wayland's Smithy, Berkshire, England. General view of the chambered long barrow. Photo: A. F. Kersting.

78 (centre) Wayland's Smithy, Berkshire, England. Capstone of a chamber being brought into position during restoration of the chambered long barrow. Photo: British Crown copyright; reproduced by permission of Her Britannic Majesty's Stationery Office.

78 (bottom) Wayland's Smithy, Berkshire, England. Facade of the chambered long barrow. Photo: British Crown copyright; reproduced by permission of Her Britannic Majesty's Stationery Office.

83 Maes Howe, Mainland, Orkney. Interior of the chamber of the passage grave. Photo: British Crown copyright; reproduced by permission of the Department of the Environment.

84 (top) Camster Round, Caithness, Scotland. General view of the passage grave. Photo: Janet Bord.

84 (bottom left) Unstan, Mainland, Ork-

ney. Interior of the stalled cairn. Photo: British Crown copyright; reproduced by permission of the Department of the Environment.

84 (bottom right) Unstan, Mainland, Orkney. Entrance to the one side-chamber of the stalled cairn. Photo: James G. Carrick.

94 Callanish, Lewis, Outer Hebrides. General view of the stone circle. Photo: Aerofilms Ltd.

98 (top left) Stonehenge, Wiltshire, England. Air view. Photo: Janet Bord and Colin Bord.

98 (top right) The Rollright Stones, Oxfordshire, England. Air view. Photo: Aerofilms Ltd.

98 (bottom left) Stonehenge, Wiltshire, England. Outer ring of the sarsen temple. Photo: Royal Commission on Historical Monuments (England).

98 (bottom right) Castlerigg, Cumbria, England. General view of the stone circle. Photo: Janet Bord.

107 Balnuaran of Clava, Inverness-shire, Scotland. The passage of one of the passage graves. Photo: Janet Bord.

109 (top) Carnac, Morbihan, France. Stone alignments. Photo: Aerofilms Ltd.

109 (bottom) Lagadyar, Finistère, France. Stone alignment. Photo by courtesy of the French Government Tourist Office.

112 (top) Stonehenge, Wiltshire, England. General view from the west. Photo: British Crown copyright; reproduced by permission of Her Britannic Majesty's Stationery Office.

112 (bottom) Stonehenge, Wiltshire, England. View from within the circle of the sun rising over the Heel stone. Photo: British Crown copyright; reproduced by permission of Her Britannic Majesty's Stationery Office.

114 (top) Stonehenge, Wiltshire, England. The inner horseshoe of trilithons. Photo: Janet Bord.

114 (centre) A sarsen stone on Marlborough Downs, England. Photo: British Crown copyright; reproduced by permission of Her Britannic Majesty's Stationery Office.

114 (bottom) Stonehenge, Wiltshire, England. Restoration work in progress. Photo: British Crown copyright; reproduced by permission of Her Britannic Majesty's Stationery Office.

115 (top) Silbury Hill, Wiltshire, England. General view. Photo: Janet Bord.

115 (bottom) Neolithic antler and bone tools from Easton Down flint mines. Salisbury and South Wiltshire Museum. Photo: Stanley Thomas.

117 Avebury, Wiltshire, England. The Kennett Avenue. Photo: Robert Estall.

127 (top) Durrington Walls, Wiltshire, England. Air view of the ditch of the henge monument and the post-holes of a roundhouse during excavation. Photo by courtesy of G. J. Wainwright.

135 (top) Archaeological excavation on a grid basis at Maiden Castle. Photo: Sir Mortimer Wheeler by courtesy of the Society of Antiquaries.

135 (bottom) Archaeological excavation by section at Maiden Castle. Photo: Sir Mortimer Wheeler by courtesy of the Society of Antiquaries.

144 (top) Part of the side of the Standard of Ur that depicts war. From the Early Dynastic cemetery at Ur, Iraq. British Museum. Photo: Phaidon Archive.

144 (bottom) Part of the side of the Standard of Ur that depicts peace. From the Early Dynastic cemetery at Ur, Iraq. British Museum. Photo: Phaidon Archive.

152 (top) Palmela, Estremadura, Portugal. View into the porthole entrance of the rock-cut tomb. Photo reproduced by permission of R. J. Harrison.

152 (centre) Nether Largie, Strathclyde, Scotland. Bronze Age cist in the north cairn. Photo: Janet Bord.

152 (bottom) Camster Round, Caithness, Scotland. General view of the passage grave. Photo: James G. Carrick.

153 (top) Bryn Celli Ddu, Anglesey, Wales. Interior of the passage grave. Photo: Janet Bord.

153 (centre) Dolmen de Mané Rutual, Morbihan, France. Exterior of the gallery grave. Photo: Robert Estall.

153 (bottom) Trethevy Quoit, Cornwall, England. General view of the chambered tomb. Photo: Janet Bord.

155 (top) Figurine of a reclining woman. From the Hypogeum, Tarxien, Malta. National Museum, Valletta. Photo: Robert Estall.

155 (bottom left) Cast of a figurine of a woman from Haġar Qim, Malta. British Museum, London. Photo by courtesy of the Trustees of the British Museum.

155 (bottom right) Carving in stone of a bull and a sow. The middle temple, Tarxien, Malta. Photo: Robert Estall.

156 (top) Decorated kerbstone in the Tarxien temple complex, Malta. Photo by courtesy of the Malta Government Tourist Office.

156 (bottom left) Decorated altar in the first temple at Tarxien, Malta. Photo: Robert Estall.

156 (bottom right) Decorated stone in the Haġar Qim temple complex, Malta. Photo by courtesy of the Malta Government Tourist Office.

164 (top left) Knowth, Co. Meath, Ireland. Exterior of a stone bowl found in the eastern passage grave. Photo: E. T. J. T. Kwint.

164 (top right) Knowth, Co. Meath, Ireland. Interior of a stone bowl found in the eastern passage grave. Photo: E. T. J. T. Kwint.

164 (bottom) Knowth, Co. Meath, Ireland. Pecked and shaded decoration in the eastern passage grave. Photo: E. T. J. T. Kwint.

167 (top left) Fussell's Lodge, Wiltshire, England. Neolithic pots from the long barrow. Salisbury and South Wiltshire Museum. Photo: Stanley Thomas.

167 (top right) Durrington Walls, Wiltshire, England. Grooved ware pot from the henge monument. Salisbury and South Wiltshire Museum. Photo: Pictorial Colour Slides.

167 (centre) Folkton Wold, Yorkshire, England. Decorated chalk 'drum' from a grave under a barrow. British Museum. Photo: Stanley Thomas.

167 (bottom right) Machrie Moor, Arran, Scotland. Skull from a short cist in the stone circle. Hunterian Museum, University of Glasgow. Photo: Euan MacKie.

167 (bottom left) Torlin, Arran, Scotland. Skull from the long cairn. Hunterian Museum, University of Glasgow. Photo: Euan MacKie.

177 Skara Brae, Mainland, Orkney. Houses 8, 2 and 1. Photo: Graham Ritchie.

181 (top left) The Avenue, Stonehenge, Wiltshire, England. Fragments of textile from a burial in an oval barrow nearby. Salisbury and South Wiltshire Museum. Photo: Stanley Thomas.

181 (top right) Borum Eshøj, Denmark. Costume of an old man from an oak coffin burial in the mound. Photo by courtesy of the National Museum, Copenhagen.

181 (bottom left) Windmill Hill, Wiltshire, England. Neolithic bone and antler tools from the causewayed camp. The Alexander Keiller Museum, Avebury. Photo: Stanley Thomas.

181 (bottom right) Skrydstrup and Egtved, Denmark. Reconstructions of girls' costumes from oak coffin burials at Skrydstrup (left) and Egtved (right). Photo: Lennart Larsen.

188 (top) Dolmen de Mané Lud, Morbihan, France. Ship carvings in the chambered tomb. Photo: Robert Estall.

188 (bottom) Herrestrup, Denmark. Ship carvings on a stone. Photo by courtesy of the National Museum, Copenhagen.

197 Agar Kuf, Iraq. Ziggurat and temple complex. Photo: Aerofilms Ltd.

198 The Kennett Avenue, Avebury, Wiltshire, England. Photo: Janet Bord.

COLOUR PHOTOGRAPHS

Page

17 Stonehenge, Wiltshire, England. A trilithon. Photo: British Crown copyright; reproduced by permission of Her Britannic Majesty's Stationery Office.

18 Skara Brae, Mainland, Orkney. House 1. Photo: Graham Ritchie.

35 Haġar Qim, Malta. Temple gateway. Photo: J. Rufus by courtesy of Robert Harding Associates.

36 Tarxien, Malta. Interior of the Hypogeum. Photo: Euan MacKie.

69 Knowth, Co. Meath, Ireland. Corbelled stone dome of the chamber of the eastern passage grave. Photo: E. T. J. T. Kwint.

70 Longhouse, Pembroke, Wales. General view of the chambered tomb. Photo: A. F. Kersting.

87 Belas Knap, Gloucestershire, England. False entrance and horned forecourt of the long chambered cairn. Photo: John Bethell.

88 West Kennett, Wiltshire, England. Interior. Photo: Michael Holford.

105 The Ballinaby Stone, Islay, Scotland. Photo: Euan MacKie.

106 Kintraw, Argyll, Scotland. View from the platform of the standing stone and the Jura hills. Photo: Euan MacKie.

123 Avebury, Wiltshire, England. Air view of the henge monument and stone circles. Photo: British Crown copyright; reproduced by permission of Her Britannic Majesty's Stationery Office.

124 Avebury, Wiltshire, England. The outer stone circle. Photo: A. F. Kersting.

141 Le Grand Menhir Brisé, Morbihan, France. Professor Alexander Thom standing at one end of the toppled megalith. Photo: A. S. Thom.

142 Carnac, Morbihan, France. Stone alignments. Photo: Michael Holford.

159 Brogar, Mainland, Orkney. The ditch of the henge monument and the stone circle. Photo: James G. Carrick.

160 Stonehenge, Wiltshire, England. Photo: Michael Holford.

Index

irrigation, influence on stratified society in Spain, 161
Islay, island of, 102

Jażdżewski, Konrad, 169
Jersey, 51, 58
Jerusalem, Solomon's Temple, 68
Jura, island of, 101, 102, 106

Keiller, Alexander, 118
Kercado, 58
Kerlescan, 108
Kermario, 108, 110
Kerugou pottery, 60
Kintraw, 102; *101*, *106*
Kintyre peninsula, 101
Kirkcudbrightshire, 62, 79, 81
Knap of Howar, 176
Knights of St. John, 25
Knowe of Craie, 86
Knowe of Yarso, 86
Knowth, 63, 64–7, 71, 74, 82, 166, 182; *65*, *69*, *73*, *164*
Kordin, 27

Lagadyar, *109*
Lagash, 191–2
Lamarck, Jean-Baptiste de Monet, Chevalier de, 133, 134, 136, 137
Lébous, 52
Leisner, Georg, 38
Leisner, Vera, 38
L'Helgouach, J., 163
Lewis, 183
Libby, W., 9, 10
limestone, building material, 27
Lisbon, 44
Lochhill, 62, 79, 81, 169
Locmariaquer, 58, 61, 110
long barrows, 7, 54, 58, 60, 113; Britain, 54, 58, 60, 75, 76–9, 163, 168, 169, 184, 185; *77*
long cairns, Britain, 76, 79–81, 184, 185; *87*, *88*; Brittany, 165; Ireland, 62–3; Scotland, 63, 75, 76, 79, 169
Longhouse, *70*
Loughcrew, 64, 71
Loughcrew ware, 71

Maes Howe, 44, 75, 85, 89–90; *83*
Maiden Castle, *135*
Malta, 182; carvings, 26–7, 28, 189; *31*, *156*, *188*; collective burial, 30, 150–1, 162; diet, 151; origins of megaliths in, 146–54; pottery, 147, 151; religion, 154; *155*; rock-cut tombs, 27, 28–30, 32, 44, 45, 147–9; *36*; temples, 25–8, 30–2, 146–54, 162, 195–6; *29*, *31*, *35*, *156*
Man, Isle of, 63, 76
Mané-Carnaplaye, 58
Mané Kerioned, 60
Mané Lud, 189; *188*
Mané Rumal, 58
Mané Rutual, *59*, *153*
Marden, 122
Marlborough Downs, 118, 120; *114*
Marseilles, 51
Marx, Karl, 133–4
Maya, 89, 128, 174
measuring systems, 68–71, 95–6, 191–2
Mediterranean, 33, 37, 44, 49, 92, 136
megalith, definition, 13
megalithic yards, 68–71, 95–6, 191–2
Le Menec, 108

menhirs, 13
Mesopotamia, boats, 187; and origins of megalith builders, 192–6, 199; *197*; technology, 137; temples, *197*; urban civilization, 136, 143, 154, 191; *144*
metal working, Anatolia, 137; Balkans, 137; Brittany, 61; Iberia, 33, 44, 48, 49–50; Tyrol, 191, 192
Mġarr, 27, 32, 147, 149, 151, 154; *29*
Mid Gleniron, 82, 86
Midhowe, 86
Los Millares, 33, 34, 42–4, 48, 49, 50, 63, 157, 158; *47*
Mnajdra, 28; *31*
Mohenjo-daro, 191, 192
Monamore, 62, 75, 76, 80–1, 169
Mont St. Michel, 60
Monts Grantez, 58
moon observatories, 99, 110, 113; *105*, *141*, *159*
Morant, G. M., 92
Morbihan, 52, 58, 60–1, 108
Mound of the Hostages, 71
Mount Pleasant, 122
Muge, 157
Murcia, 41
Musson, C. M., 126
Mycenaean culture, 122, 150

Netherlands, 140
Nether Largie, *152*
New Grange, 63, 64, 67–71, 74, 184, 187; *72*, *73*; carvings, 24; midwinter sunrise at, 68, 108, 196; *72*; stone circle, 108, 182–3, 185, 192
Nile delta, 143
North Africa, 49, 92, 161, 162

O'Kelly, Brian, 67, 68
Oporto, 189
Orkneys, chambered cairns, 182, 184; passage graves, 34, 44, 75, 85–90, 172; *83*; pottery, 168; *167*; stalled cairn, 75; *84*; stone circle, *159*; *see also* Skara Brae
orthostats, 13

Palestine, 143, 154
Palmela, *152*
Papa Westray, 86–9, 176
passage graves, 8, 13, 33, 44; *11*; Brittany, 34, 52–61, 63, 66, 75, 85, 162–5; *53*, *55*, *56*, *59*; links with stone circles, 182–3; France, 51–61, 162–5; *53*, *55*, *56*, *59*; Iberia, 34, 38–44, 50, 52, 54, 58, 63, 74, 75, 154, 157–62; *43*; Ireland, 44, 52, 58, 60, 61, 62–74, 75, 85, 158, 165–6, 182–3; *65*, *69*, *164*; Orkney, 44; Scotland, 44, 52, 58, 60, 67, 75–6, 81–9, 104–8, 182–3; *83*, *84*, *107*, *153*; Wales, 76, 81, 85; *70*
Penedo de Lexim, 50
Peru, 192
Petit Mont, 189
Petrie, George, 15
Piggott, Stuart, 22, 91
Pimperne, 169
Ploudalmezeau, 57
Poço da Gateira, 38
Polynesia, 147
portal dolmens, 76, 169
Portugal, *see* Iberia
pot boilers, 19
pottery, Beaker pottery, 46, 48, 50, 57, 58, 119, 122, 158; Cardial, 34–7, 51, 157; *39*; Chasseyan, 60; *copos* ware, 45–6, 48, 186;

207